HOW TO RECOVER FROM PET BUSINESS BURNOUT

Reclaim Your Personal Life, Combat Compassion Fatigue, and Create Work/Life Balance While Running Your Pet Sitting, Dog Walking, Dog Training, or Pet Grooming Business

KRISTIN MORRISON

OTHER BOOKS BY KRISTIN MORRISON:

Six-Figure Pet Sitting:
Catapult Your Pet Sitting Business
to Unlimited Success

Six-Figure Pet Business:
Unleash the Potential in Your Dog Training,
Pet Grooming, and Doggy Day Care Business

Prosperous Pet Business:
Interviews with the Experts

30 Days to Start and Grow
Your Pet Sitting and Dog Walking Business:
A Step-By-Step Guide to Launch, Attract Clients,
and Make a Profit

The Hiring Handbook
for Pet Sitters and Dog Walkers:
How to Find, Hire, and Keep the Best Staff for
Your Pet Sitting and Dog Walking Business

HOW TO RECOVER FROM PET BUSINESS BURNOUT

"Kristin Morrison has done it again! The How to Recover from Pet Business Burnout *book will greatly improve so many lives. A must-read by all business owners. I can't wait to put all this in practice myself!"*

Jessica Abernathy
President of National Association of Professional
Pet Sitters (NAPPS)

"Burnout is real! I know firsthand how serious this is, as I have personally grappled with burnout-induced clinical depression. Kristin brilliantly sheds light on this potentially debilitating symptom of perfectionism, the "do it all syndrome" and workaholism. Every entrepreneur will identify with every chapter of the book How to Recover from Pet Business Burnout. *More importantly, Kristin provides simple and actionable strategies to help any entrepreneur on the path to recovery or prevent you from traveling down a path towards burnout."*

Gila Kurtz
President and Co-Founder of
Dog is Good

"Kristin's latest book is a must-have for anyone feeling burned out or depleted in their pet business. Whether you are struggling with time management, work/life balance or finances, you can start using the practical and actionable steps at the end of each chapter today."

Kimberly Kester
Best Friends Dog Walking & Pet Resort
Vineland, Ontario, Canada

"Flexibility is one of many benefits of owning your own company, but it can quickly become a curse as every hour of your day fills with work. Few authors address the very real issue of burnout. With over twenty-five years in the pet care industry, author and pet business coach Kristin Morrison provides hard-earned advice for how to craft a business that doesn't sacrifice your sanity or your bottom line. How to Recover from Pet Business Burnout covers what burnout is, how it happens, and provides a comprehensive, step-by-step guide to fostering work/life balance. Reclaim your life and reignite your love for your pet business, one page at a time."

Pet Sitters Associates, LLC
Business Insurance for Pet Care Providers

"Wow! I can't say enough great things about How to Recover from Pet Business Burnout. Kristin not only addresses what to do if you are currently experiencing burnout, but also how to prevent burnout from happening. Kristin's book has been a game-changer for me and gives me the tools to live a better life. I will definitely be recommending it to all of my pet business friends. I honestly do not think you can balance a successful business and personal life without the information in this book!"

Heidi Lewis
Heidi & Hope Pet Services, LLC
Naples, Florida

"This book could not have come at a better time for me, personally and professionally. A few pages into reading How to Recover from Pet Business Burnout, I was hooked! It was as if Kristin was speaking directly to me. I began to understand why I was feeling so withdrawn and overwhelmed at the same time. Not only was I experiencing all the hardships of the pandemic, but I was in complete 'burnout mode' without realizing it. Through new ideas on how to run my business and not let it run me, self-care tips and ways to calm my inner self, I can now see a light at the end of the tunnel. For me, the most important parts of this book were letting go of negative beliefs and learning to incorporate affirmations to get the things I desire. My personal and professional life feel back on track again."

LaDonna Madden
Rocky Top Pet Services
Maryville, Tennessee

"Kristin Morrison's newest book is an unparalleled masterpiece that will end up on shelves next to books like Napoleon Hill's Think and Grow Rich, and The 7 Habits of Highly Effective People by Stephen R. Covey. Nowhere have I seen so much practical, helpful information about gaining control of your own personal self, your habits and your choices, all in one place. This book is a necessity for all who feel overwhelmed, disillusioned or are floundering in trying to design or redesign their life so that it can carry them to their goals. Opening your heart and mind to new ideas, following the guidelines and Action Steps and being willing to spend some time making real changes to the way you think truly can help you get out of your funk, and begin powerfully moving toward your goals, whatever they may be!"

Dee Kate Murdock
Leash and Collar Pet Care
Lubbock, Texas

"After I started my pet business, I lost track of my daily meditation routines and let my business take control over my life. I don't have a personal/family/ friend life anymore. I am ready to take back control and give myself 'me' time. I am happy Kristin reminded me about how important it is to live, practice and implement the mind, body and spirit bond on a daily basis."

MJ Gonzalez
Pets By MJ
San Diego, California

"My burnout was translating to my clients as a lack of passion for my profession, which is absolutely not true! How to Recover from Pet Business Burnout gave me the perspective, tools, inspiration and compassion I needed for my recovery. During my journey, I learned that my business cannot thrive, let alone survive, without self-care. Also, I am more than just my business and my self-worth is not dependent on my success. I am extremely excited for the future where I have a business that works for me and not the other way around."

Melinda Meltzer
Stay and Play Pet Sitting, Inc.
Temecula, California

"Kristin allows you into her own personal burnout experience and gives you the inside view on proven techniques that can work for you. Even if you take just one thing away from this book and work on that, you and your pet business will be better off. I am already working on putting things into place to ensure my business success. Do not pass this book up if you are experiencing burnout!"

Alicia Becker
North Metro Pet Services, LLC
Thornton, Colorado

"I loved the book's Action Steps. Through these, Kristin provided a variety of tasks, depending on how you want to fix your burnout. I have realized that I need to work on my business and also myself, so I can successfully keep my business running without feeling burnout. Hearing from other pet care providers in each chapter was very encouraging and helped me understand I am not the only one going through this. I highly recommend reading the book and taking the time to follow the Action Steps and journaling prompts."

Josie Kropp
Simply Pets Pet Sitting, LLC
St. Charles, Illinois

"If you're experiencing burnout with your pet service business, I encourage you to buy this book. Take the basics of all the self-help books you've read (or want to read!), roll them all together, and you have Kristin Morrison's How to Recover from Pet Business Burnout. *Kristin lays out the recipe to recover from pet business burnout and improve your life. I've always felt I was being a baby about needing adequate sleep, healthy eating habits, daily exercise and a balanced life in order to function properly. Kristin's book validated my needs and gave me permission to do these things for myself. After reading this gem and working through the exercises and action items, I'm already experiencing the benefits of burnout recovery!"*

Janet Reed, PhD
Dr. J's Pet Services, LLC
Austin, Texas

"Every single word in this book spoke to my soul. How ironic that I needed to read a book to teach me to take time to read a book! I knew something was awry in my business and personal life, but I didn't know what. Reading this book helped me see I had lost all of the boundaries I had worked so hard to establish. The information gained by reading it will help my business, my personal life and (most importantly) my marriage. I hope to be in a different place by this time next year — I believe I can achieve this balance because of Kristin and the book How to Recover from Pet Business Burnout.*"*

Colleen Sheffield Greene
Colleen Takes on the Sitting World
Savannah, Georgia

"As pet business owners, this book helped us gain a clearer understanding of our business and personal life priorities. It is full of practical action steps that allow you to discover not only the signs of burnout, but also how to recover from it and avoid it entirely. By taking a holistic approach and keeping the long term in perspective, Kristin has helped us to see how to acknowledge and overcome burnout so we can continue doing the work we are so passionate about. Whether three months or 30 years in, the topic of burnout is something we can all learn more about!"

Meghan and Collin Funkhouser
Pet Sitter Confessional Podcast

"I got so caught up in reading How to Recover from Pet Business Burnout, *and the many ways to recover from business burnout, that I decided to read the book twice! This book has given me a lot of food for thought, and I can't wait to start putting the steps into practice. Until reading this book, I hadn't realized how negative beliefs have impacted my business growth and my personal mindset. I'm looking forward to re-reading this book a third time and incorporating the steps into both my business and personal life. I especially enjoyed Kristin's personal accounts of how burnout impacted her life and the changes she made to overcome burnout. I would definitely give this book five stars!"*

Nancy Mercurio
No Place Like Home Pet Sitting & Dog Walking
Haddon Heights, New Jersey

"I left my corporate job and started my own pet care company to improve my quality of life. Even though my business is doing fine, I have recently been feeling somewhat lost and adrift. Kristin's book is just what I needed. Each chapter provides practical suggestions for taking steps to feel more in control of yourself and your business and also includes great stories from others who have also been through burnout and made it to the other side. Having read the book and worked on several of the Action Steps, I can say that I'm feeling more refreshed and hopeful than I have in months. Thank you, Kristin!"

Susan Hurst
Susan Sits Pets
Wilmington, Delaware

"This book absolutely could not have come at a better time! I was starting to feel like I was really struggling. I had already tried putting some steps in place to help, but I have found this book is really encouraging me to make positive changes and has given me some ideas I wouldn't have even thought of otherwise.

I love how each chapter offers something different to consider and how each Action Step is clearly laid out and easy to follow. I also feel comforted reading the stories from Kristin and other pet professionals; it's really nice to know I'm not alone!

I have already started implementing some of Kristin's suggestions, after months of feeling burned out, and I feel like I am starting to de-stress and gain better insight into how to best help myself... and in turn, how to help my clients even more. Thank you, Kristin!"

Kirsty Everard
Kirsty's Paws
Bournemouth, England

How to Recover from Pet Business Burnout: Reclaim Your Personal Life, Combat Compassion Fatigue, and Create Work/Life Balance While Running Your Pet Sitting, Dog Walking, Dog Training, or Pet Grooming Business

This book is dedicated to those suffering from overworking and underliving.

May these pages provide you with peace and clarity to create a new path forward.

Table of Contents

Before You Begin...

What you are holding in your hands is not some accidental, untested information on how to recover from pet business burnout.

The information you are about to read is, unfortunately, hard won. This book came to be because of my profound need to deal with — and ultimately cure — my own business burnout... burnout I should have seen coming because I had been through it before. In fact, earlier burnout had almost caused me to walk away from my business altogether.

If you had asked me many years ago if I had solved my challenges around business burnout, I would have unequivocally said, "Yes." However, if you had asked me that same question a couple of years ago, I would have sadly said, "No." My business had changed form and shape since my last burnout triage, and because of those changes, there was more recovery work for me to do.

During my last bout of burnout, I looked for a book to walk me through the process of recovery. I found some books that touched on various ways of coping with burnout and I was grateful for them (you'll find them listed in the *Reading List* at the end of the book), but what I was searching for was a comprehensive, step-by-step guidebook that would take me from feeling overwhelmed and exhausted to energetic and enthusiastic. I wanted to fall in love with my business and life again.

When I couldn't find the book that I hoped would lead me to a full recovery from business burnout, I decided that once I got to a place of recovery, balance and peace in my business and my life again, I would then write a book to help others who were struggling. These chapters contain the same steps I took to relieve my own suffering of the seemingly insurmountable stress that can come from being a business owner and entrepreneur.

But before I walk you through the process of healing my own burnout, I want to share some of my backstory:

In my mid-20s, I started my first business: a pet sitting and dog walking business that combined my love of animals and my desire to be my own boss.

When I first started my pet business, I felt excited and motivated to push past my daily exhaustion in order to grow my business as quickly as possible. Growing my first business was a grueling process and I found myself tired at the end of most days, even though I barely had any clients!

Within a few years, however, that business did what most business owners want their business to do—it became wildly successful. I had more clients than I could reasonably manage, even though I had hired many people to help me with the various services my business provided our clients. I had to turn a lot of clients away. It was a "good problem" to have, but I found myself stressed a lot of the time.

Friends and family would often compliment me on my business success, and my ego *really* liked hearing that they thought of me as successful. Being busy and being perceived by others as a successful business owner made me feel important and valued. But the truth was that I didn't feel successful. Stress was the byproduct of my success and no amount of praise from others could take away the sheer exhaustion that came from living a life out of balance week after week.

To the outside world, I looked like I had it all together. In reality, the very success that I had longed for, and had now achieved, was causing me stress and pain.

I remember looking at my overloaded calendar and lengthy to-do list and feeling frustrated that I couldn't find time in my busy schedule to buy new clothes for a work event. I didn't even have time to spend the money I had earned! That moment was one of the many wake-up calls I received that highlighted my need to deal with burnout.

This was not the life I wanted to live. In fact, if this was what being a "successful business owner" was, I wanted out! However, when I thought about what I would do for work if I quit running my business, I had no idea. I loved the freedom and autonomy of being self-employed. I just didn't like feeling that I always had to be busy doing tasks to keep my business going or the stress and strain that surrounded me on a daily (and sometimes minute-to-minute) basis.

So, one day, in the midst of yet another busy day (they were all busy days back then), I forced myself to be still and quiet in order to reflect consciously upon the state of my business and my life. In that moment of self-reflection, I had a powerful realization: my true definition of success meant having both time *and* money.

I was stressed when I had a lot of time but no clients early in my business, and here I was again, equally stressed with plenty of clients but no time. I wanted to create a work and personal life that gave me both. I knew I needed to radically shift my business in order to reduce work stress and create more time and space in my personal life. *But how?*

I had no idea what "radical changes" I'd need to make, but I decided to give myself the time limit of one year to change the way I ran my business. I decided that, if at the end of those 365 days, I didn't have both time and money, I would sell the business or simply walk away.

A year later, I had completely transformed my work life. Instead of working seven days a week, I was only working three days a week. But even more surprising was that in my Year of Radical Change (yes, the year has a name; it deserved one!), I made nearly *double the profit* of what I'd made working seven days a week.

In the following chapters, you'll read about what exactly I did to create that profound shift, but more importantly, *who I had to become for it to happen.* Changing my business was not enough because radical shifts do not happen in a vacuum. In order to make lasting change in one part of my life, what existed around it also needed to shift. My business had to change. I had to change. In that year, both my business and I did change, and we both changed for the better.

Was that transformation an easy process? Definitely not. First, as is often the case with major changes, I had to admit that there was a problem. Then, I had to be willing to change (something humans— including this human—resist). Bringing about that change required consistently choosing curiosity and creativity over fear when it came to new ways of running the business. It required me to choose a new life rather than the old life that, though tattered and exhausting, was familiar. I didn't know who I'd be at the end of my Year of Radical Change... and you might not either.

Since 2000, I have coached many business owners through their own burnout recovery processes. I know that the solutions you're about to read work. Not only have they worked for me, but they have worked well for many other business owners from across the world whom I have coached through their own burnout recoveries.

However, because each person and stressful situation are unique, not *everything* contained in the book will lead to your burnout cure.

But, if you open your mind and give some of your precious time to practicing what you learn in this book, you will find at least some of the tools, ideas and information contained in this book — and perhaps even most of it — will help you. When it comes to recovering from burnout, "at least some" can be enough to rekindle your passion for your business and ultimately free up your time, as well as help you fall in love with your business — and your life — again.

It did for me. My intention in writing the steps contained in this book is that each one will help you have a similar experience with your own life and business.

One more thought before I set you free to dive into this book and create your own Radical Change:

I assumed I'd been cured from burnout forever after I transformed my service-based business and my life. And yet, years later, I again experienced crippling burnout.

For a number of years after I'd made my business changes, my time and energy were renewed. Burnout was a distant memory. I eventually sold my pet care business and focused my time on writing books, coaching, speaking at events and leading webinars, recording my podcast and other projects. Selling my business enabled me to focus on being the captain of my ship and to be able to use my time as an entrepreneur however I saw fit, even more than when I'd been at the helm of my service-based business.

But gradually, my schedule as an entrepreneur began to get busier and busier and, without my realizing it at first, that familiar stress and a lack of time began creeping up again. Then something really wonderful happened, but it was the straw that broke the burnout camel's back.

One day, out of the blue, I got a call from a reporter from a well-known online publication. He wrote an article about my business. That interview went viral and as a result, I was invited to be interviewed on TV shows all over the country, and on podcasts and a lot of other media. My already cramped schedule began to be squeezed from all of this business success. (Yes, there is that "success" word again.)

Getting national and international publicity is what most entrepreneurs and business owners dream about, right? It was certainly my dream. I loved the publicity (and still love it!), but I found it ironic that the very success that I wanted — this time in the form of publicity, speaking engagements and interviews — was once again creating stress and strain on my time, my business and my personal life.

Knowing I needed to regroup and recharge, I dove once again into the process of recovery. I read books and articles searching for a cure to this version of my burnout and implemented a lot of what had worked years before in my service-based business into my new life as an entrepreneur. I discussed burnout with many business owners and entrepreneurs to determine what worked for them when it came to burnout recovery (and what didn't), regardless of whether they were service-based business owners, entrepreneurs or immersed in the corporate world. I also engaged in "burnout recovery experiments" and deep discussions with my husband, who, at the time, was an overworked corporate attorney experiencing his own version of burnout.

And now, as you begin your journey to burnout recovery, I invite you to open your mind — and your heart — and step into your own Radical Change. It's my intention that you will find your business and your personal life are changed for the better after reading this book.

How to Use This Book

In the pages that follow, I will show you how to prevent burnout. I will also show you how to heal if you already have the crippling burnout that is all too common among entrepreneurs, business owners and innovators. These chapters will help you overcome your own exhaustion and launch your own Radical Change. It will take effort on your part to do the self-reflection and make the radical changes that this book encourages, but I promise, *it will be worth it.*

Each chapter of this book will give you actionable suggestions (some practical, others more unexpected) for overcoming burnout and finding your own balance. I encourage you to flip through the contents and pick out the sections that appeal most to you. Although each part of the book is important for your journey, you do not need to start with Chapter One if your most pressing need today is somewhere else in the book.

I will also share more specific parts of my own story at the end of each chapter so you can learn from my hard-won experiences healing from burnout. At the end of each chapter, you will find *Action Steps* that match the topic and content with concrete, measurable steps you can take to apply the chapter's lessons to your life and business right away. Reading each chapter will likely give you some relief, but the true cure will be found in the *Action Steps* at the end of each chapter.

I am not the only one whose stories you will find in this book. Inevitably in interviews or social engagements, colleagues, family and friends ask, "What book are you working on next?" When I mentioned the topic of burnout, so many said, "I need help with that!" I've also discussed burnout recovery strategies and challenges with a number of pet business owners in the course of writing this book. Many of their stories will be in this book as *Burnout Recovery Success Stories*. These are real-life entrepreneurs and business owners who have been where you are now and have successfully recovered from their own burnout.

They have generously shared their stories in order to help you recover.

Finally, at the end of the book, you will find *Recommended Resources* and a *Reading List* to help you maintain your momentum and progress after you have finished the final *Action Step*.

Now that you know what to expect from this book, it's time to get started! Here are the very first foundational *Action Steps* to take before you begin with Chapter One:

Action Step

Designate a special journal or notebook for taking notes and completing the *Action Steps* and other exercises in this book. This "burnout recovery journal" will be an important part of your journey while you read this book and afterwards. Avoiding burnout is an ongoing process. Organizing your thoughts and realizations in one place will be a source of motivation that you can return to again and again when you need a reminder of the things you learned from this book.

Action Step

Some of the *Action Steps* in this book will require that you use a timer. If you do not have a timer you can use while you work through this book, purchase a new one for that purpose. Even though phones come with timers built in, I recommend using a separate timer so you do not get distracted by texts, phone calls or social media while you work. Part of recovering from (and later, preventing) burnout will be setting boundaries and focusing on one task at a time, starting with how you keep track of time for the assignments in this book. It may seem like a small detail, but separating your timer from the distractions that come along with your phone is more important than you might realize. On that note, I recommend that you put your phone in another room while you're reading this book and doing the *Action Steps*, if at all possible. This will help you focus on you, your business and your life without distraction.

Action Step

Join the private Facebook group for readers of *How to Recover from Pet Business Burnout* at www.Facebook.com/groups/RecoverFromPet-BusinessBurnout to connect with other readers, share ideas and celebrate your progress.

Introduction

Why Business Burnout Happens

*"These mountains that you were carrying,
you were only supposed to climb."*

–Najwa Zebian

Since you picked up this book, you are likely already aware that you are at risk or are already experiencing business burnout. Maybe you already feel buried in stress, or you can feel the beginnings of burnout stirring as responsibility piles on, or you deal with daily or weekly "business fires" that need putting out. But, if by chance you are wondering if the steps you'll find in this book are really for you, read on. The information contained here is about identifying why and how business burnout happens and what the biggest risks are *for you*. In this book, I'll present many solutions for burnout recovery. You may wish to work through each step to find relief, or you may pick and choose the suggestions that resonate best with you and your current needs. The more you can make your burnout recovery address your unique life and business, the more successful it will be. Understanding what is causing your personal burnout and how your specific tendencies and situation contribute to business burnout will help you personalize your recovery journey.

Five Signs You May Be Suffering from Burnout

Burnout is different from person to person, but there are some warning signs I have seen in myself and in my coaching clients who are experiencing burnout. You may, like many of my clients, find that all five of these are true for you. Or you may only see yourself in two or three of these signs but recognize that they are serious enough to warrant concern.

Read through this list of the five most common signs you may need to recover from business burnout and evaluate how many are true for you:

- **You no longer feel the joy and creativity you once had.**
  Most entrepreneurs and business owners are, by nature, excited about their ventures. You wouldn't have made it as far as you have in your career with animals without that passion. However, when exhaustion and frustration creep in and stay for a while, work can become a grind instead of a joy. If cynicism, fatigue or annoyance are replacing what used to be passion for your work, it is time to put your immediate focus on burnout recovery.

- **Your family and friends complain you are always working.**
  You may not be able to see that you're in the throes of burnout yet, but your friends and family may be able to see what you can't. If you ask those closest to you, would they say you have a healthy work/life balance? Or would they say you are often on your phone or computer, dealing with work, instead of present and attentive to life outside of work? Phone and computer work are necessary and needed, but so is your ability to focus on life's important moments without the constant interruption of work. If you are missing that balance between the two, you will probably benefit from the content of this book.

- **You are exhausted or sick more often than you used to be.**
  Even if you are determined to push through and keep working, your body will eventually force you to slow down. We all feel more tired some days than others, but chronic exhaustion is something else entirely. Frequent or persistent tiredness or illness can be a sign that you are burned out.

- **You constantly multitask, including during your free time.**
  When was the last time you watched a movie or went out with friends and did not check your work messages? How often is your time off spent worrying about work or dreading what might be happening in your absence? If the time you carve out

for yourself is full of business stress, you will never be able to fully recharge, leading to deep exhaustion and burnout. The longer you go without recharging, the longer it will take to recover.

- **New ideas and opportunities bring you stress instead of excitement.**
  One of the many gifts of being an entrepreneur is being able to tap into and use creativity and vision as you lead your company. However, that creativity takes a certain amount of mental and emotional space; it cannot be rushed or forced. If a new idea or unexpected opportunity just makes you tired instead of exciting you like it may have previously, this may be a warning sign that you need to make at least some of the changes that you'll discover in this book. If you do not have the energy for exploring new ideas or opportunities, you are probably already burned out.

Even initially exciting and wonderful opportunities can sometimes lead to burnout if we're not vigilant. As I mentioned in the Before You Begin section of this book, it was the fantastic opportunity of a viral article about me and my business (which led to a lot more publicity than I was accustomed to) and the busy schedule which accompanied it that alerted me to the fact that I was experiencing yet another round of burnout. Even though it was often fun and exciting to be interviewed on TV, magazines, podcasts and other media, it was also exhausting. The interviews were piling up as fast as they were coming in and I was not giving myself the necessary time and space in between the media interviews to recharge.

> IF YOU DO NOT HAVE THE ENERGY FOR EXPLORING NEW IDEAS OR OPPORTUNITIES, YOU ARE PROBABLY ALREADY BURNED OUT.

Identify What Is Causing YOUR Burnout

Burnout can, and does, happen to most people, but business owners and entrepreneurs are especially susceptible because of the highly demanding nature of being self-employed. Many of us are extremely passionate and dedicated to our careers, but that passion often comes with a cost—we take on extra responsibility and stress in our efforts to keep the business up and running, and because of that, we may find ourselves working a lot more than we would if (or when) we worked for someone else. The very nature of running a business—and especially a pet care business—often means that you find yourself spending more time on your work than a 9-5 employee.

> **Burnout Recovery Tip:**
> Tailoring your burnout recovery plan to fit your own causes of burnout and goals for recovery will make the entire process smoother and longer lasting. Throughout this book, I will give you specific questions to answer and ideas to consider. The more you apply these questions and ideas to your own situation and needs, the better your recovery will be.

Some aspects of burnout recovery are often the same across the board for all those suffering from burnout. However, you'll want to create your own specific burnout recovery plan for the most efficient path to recovery.

In order to craft your own plan from the information gleaned from this book, you'll first want to identify what is causing your specific burnout so you can tailor your recovery journey to your specific needs:

- **You are constantly working to get more clients.**
  In the early days of running a business, it may seem like the hustle to find and keep clients never ends. Unfortunately, this same struggle can come up again when you need to rebuild your client list after it dwindles—for example, after an economic recession or if many of your clients move away. After being in business for a few years, you may find you don't need to work quite so hard to bring on new clients. By that point, however, you may be deep in the throes of burnout because of the time and work it took to build your client base and because, when you're experiencing burnout, caring for those new clients may feel exhausting.

- **You are dealing with an emergency, challenge or trauma.**
  Sometimes, events outside of our control demand our full attention. For example, events like the COVID-19 pandemic

changed what a typical workday looked like for many people, seemingly overnight. Many business owners watched the situation change daily, while wondering what toll the pandemic would have on their businesses and health. Through no fault of their own, they found themselves dealing with symptoms of emotional burnout that might be different from those caused by overworking: lack of enthusiasm, difficulty focusing on business or personal matters, or crippling fear about the uncertain future. Whether it's a family emergency, a chronic or unexpected illness, or a tragedy that deeply affects you, the emotional and mental toll of unexpected emergencies can send you into burnout.

- **You are doing all (or most of) the work yourself.**
  If you haven't yet hired staff, you are likely still doing all of the pet care and office work yourself. Or, if you have hired staff members but they require a lot of ongoing instruction or handholding from you, you are forced to stay involved in the work they do, in addition to managing your own business tasks. Having staff who are unable to self-manage often defeats the purpose of hiring because you rarely get a much-needed break—the break that you assumed you'd get by hiring staff. The need to "babysit" your staff can often be more frustrating and draining than simply doing the work yourself.

- **You do not take time to recharge (or perhaps even know how to do so).**
  I understand how demanding it can be to start and run a business, but you absolutely must disconnect from work for at least some time each day or you will run yourself (and your business) into the ground. If nearly every part of your day is connected to work in some way, burnout will likely be on its way. If you have no idea how to recharge, don't worry! You'll find many ideas and suggestions for rest, renewal and rejuvenation in the coming pages of this book.

- **Business administration is taking too much of your energy.**
  When I was starting out in my own pet care business, I really enjoyed interacting with clients on the phone and through

email. As my business became more successful, however, returning phone calls and emails became one of the most stressful and time-consuming business tasks. That constant need to be returning calls and emails, combined with all the time spent invoicing and bookkeeping, left me feeling like all I did was office work. I had started my pet business because I enjoyed working with pets and their people, not to be stuck behind a computer all day. If administration details are taking a lot of your focus and life energy, they are likely contributing to your burnout.

- **You spend too much time dealing with difficult clients and/or staff.**
  In many service-based professions, difficult clients are called "vampire clients" because they suck the energy out of everything you do. If you are spending most of your time dealing with a small percentage of your clients or staff who are causing the most problems, they will contribute to business burnout and keep you from dedicating the majority of your time and focus to your other clients and ideas. When I looked closely at my own client list, I found that a handful of my clients were incredibly challenging to work with and were using up about 90% of my energy. That only left a small portion of my effort for the rest of my clients. I needed to release those challenging clients from my business to free up my time and energy. When I did, I felt so much relief and freedom! If you've got difficult clients or staff, you'll learn how to release them in the coming pages of this book.

This list of burnout causes is by no means complete, but it should at least give you an idea of some of your possible burnout risks and causes. Identifying what is causing your specific burnout will help you personalize your recovery journey to make your healing as effective and long-lasting as it can be.

Action Steps – Why Business Burnout Happens

Action Step

Before moving on to Chapter One, consider the signs and causes of burnout listed in this introduction. What hit closest to home? In your burnout recovery journal, make a list of which signs, examples and causes of burnout you see in yourself. You can refer to the examples in this introduction or add personal burnout causes you've noticed in your own life. Having this list to refer back to as you read the book will help you personalize your recovery journey and design a plan that will conquer your own specific business burnout.

Action Step

Using the list of burnout warning signs you made in the previous *Action Step*, highlight or put stars next to the examples and warning signs causing you the most difficulty in this immediate moment. Doing so will allow you to focus on those first as you begin your burnout recovery journey.

Part One

Laying the Groundwork for Transformation

"We delight in the beauty of the butterfly but rarely admit the changes it has gone through to achieve that beauty."

–Maya Angelou

ONE

Root Out Negative Beliefs

Harness Your Mindset to Cultivate a Better Relationship with Your Pet Business

"Until you make the unconscious conscious, it will direct your life and you will call it fate."

–Carl Jung

You may be thinking, "Why are we starting with a chapter about negative beliefs?" Or you might look at the table of contents and wonder, "Why is there a chapter on 'imagination' in a burnout recovery book? Shouldn't we be diving into business automation, hiring and other tangible and solid steps that will help me have more time and a personal life again? Hello?! Kristin?!"

I hear you.

I will get to those solid, tangible steps in coming chapters. But here's the thing: As I mentioned in the first pages and introduction, there are going to be some parts of this book where you will need to have an open mind and heart.

These next three chapters especially will require you to have an open mind and heart.

Before you can begin transforming your business and your life (and transformation is required if you're suffering from burnout), something else has to happen first before true and lasting change can take place in your business or your life... and that "something" comes down to mindset.

I am going to share something about myself that, at first, may seem like it has nothing to do with burnout or running a business at all, but

I believe it will help you understand what I mean when I say that your mindset needs to change before anything else can.

On January 1, 2013, I woke up realizing that I had invested a lot of time and energy into my business but hadn't invested much into what was my heart's biggest desire — to meet and marry a wonderful man.

I came to the realization that, in the same way investing time, money and energy in my business had reaped results, I likely needed to invest time, money and energy into dating if I wanted to find my right partner.

At that point, I had done a lot of prior work on my own recovery from burnout, including delegating and hiring managers, which freed up time and energy for my personal life. However, before I could put myself out there in the dating world, I knew I needed to address a lot of negative beliefs I had that would stop me before I'd even begun dating. One of the negative beliefs I had was "I'm too old to get married."

It felt vulnerable to articulate that negative belief, even to myself! However, I knew from my own burnout recovery work that if I didn't first acknowledge the negative beliefs that were standing in my way, I wouldn't be able to transform those limiting beliefs, which would likely keep me from meeting and marrying the right person.

And here's the thing, just like burnout is an often-accepted symptom of being a business owner, society as a whole tends to buy into this "too old" belief when it comes to marriage (think about all the articles and statistics about the likelihood of women over the age of 40 getting married). I was not only dealing with my own negative belief about my age, which was a very strong belief, but I was also dealing with a societal belief. These societal beliefs are often deeply rooted and can take a lot of energy and motivation to stand up to — and walk away from — in order to create a completely different reality.

After I realized that I had the belief "I'm too old to get married," I decided to do something counterintuitive. I flipped the belief on its side and explored the possibility of its polar opposite: "I'm the perfect age to get married." At first, this new belief felt like a lie because I didn't believe it yet. But then I began imagining what life would be like if this belief was true, and I began to see that many of my life experiences until that very moment had led me to a readiness to meet my partner. For example, how I'd had a lot of solitude in my life and perhaps now was the right time to transform that solitude and live my life with a special someone.

Nearly nine months after working with my negative beliefs and adjusting my perspective, on August 31, 2013, I went on my first date with my now husband!

So, what does a story about getting married have to do with recovering from burnout? Here's the connection: Without adjusting your mindset to allow the meaningful changes that are about to occur, any changes you make are less likely to stick. Your perception of the world has power over every aspect of your life and business; and, without even realizing it, you may be holding on to beliefs that are keeping you from moving to a place of healing, change and recovery. Now is the time for you to take a step back in order to evaluate and change your state of mind before you jump to making specific, tangible changes in your business.

> WITHOUT EVEN REALIZING IT, YOU MAY BE HOLDING ON TO BELIEFS THAT ARE KEEPING YOU FROM MOVING TO A PLACE OF HEALING, CHANGE AND RECOVERY.

Break Down Mental Blocks with the Power of Choice

As I was reflecting on my own burnout recovery journey and how getting in touch with my negative beliefs and mindset was really the first step toward recovery for me, I realized that I needed to start this book by helping you uncover your own mental and emotional blocks — hidden blocks that you may not even know you have. Why? Discovering your hidden (or perhaps not so hidden) blocks may unlock a whole new experience for you which can lead to rest, renewal and freedom from stress and burnout. It certainly did for me, and I'm confident that if you have commitment, focus and desire for change, it can for you, too.

In my own relentless desire to find out how to create more time and reclaim my personal life, I realized my experience of having very little time and being so stressed and overworked in my business was really a symptom of a deeper issue, rather than the crux of the problem.

Initially, I pointed my finger to the fact that I had no time, no personal life and was stressed all the time. I tried to figure out what I could do to create more time, have a personal life again and lower my stress. However, because I was simply dealing with the symptoms rather than the underlying issues, I could do all the business automation, hire the best staff and many other "action steps" but *still* be in a place of having no time and no life. My desperation caused me to explore nontraditional ways of changing my business. I will be sharing some of those methods in this chapter. The "gift" of desperation eventually served me well, and perhaps your desperation will assist you, too.

If you've tried to find a cure for your business burnout and it hasn't yet worked, perhaps your own frustration will help you realize that you have nothing to lose by simply trying what is outlined in this chapter.

Let's do it. Are you ready? Here we go.

My Negative Beliefs and How They Impacted My Life

You may have read about how I dismantled some of my negative beliefs in *Six-Figure Pet Sitting* or *Six-Figure Pet Business*. Even if you have read about how I transformed my negative beliefs in one of those books, I encourage you to read this chapter all the way through because I truly believe the work I've done to uproot and change those negative beliefs has been instrumental in my business success, as well as in my own burnout recovery.

When I thought about what defined business success for me, my definition of success was having both money *and* time. I knew a lot of business owners who had either one or the other, but I didn't know anyone who had a business that gave them both. I wanted both, but I had no clue how to create that. Even when I had a large staff, I was still working many hours and somehow not making much money. This lack of time and money, in spite of all the hours I spent working, was perplexing to me. I wanted my business to support me to create both of those valuable resources, but I couldn't see a way to achieve that goal.

What I didn't realize is that I had deeply embedded negative beliefs that had created an equally embedded negative neural pathway in my brain. As a result, those negative beliefs impaired both my thinking and actions. They also left me feeling hopeless. How was it that I was a smart and savvy business owner who had all these staff members working for me, but I still felt like I had to work so much and wasn't making much money?

I have a daily morning journal writing practice (you can read more about that in Chapter Eleven) that has led me to many important realizations. One morning, I was writing about all the stress I was experiencing as a result of working so hard in my business. I was perplexed that I could work so hard and somehow not make very much money. I was exhausted and had no idea what to do next to shift this experience, since it seemed I'd tried everything at that point.

That morning, I began to get curious about this in my writing. I reflected on how and why I was working so hard. I had thought about this numerous times in the past, since working hard and being stressed was an ongoing issue, but this particular time, I attempted to distill my experience down to the root. What was the origin of my overwork and exhaustion?

Like I mentioned at the beginning of this chapter, I'd done belief-busting work successfully on a few issues in my personal life, so I knew that to truly begin to dismantle and change a negative belief into a positive one, I had to get to the root of the issue. I realized that beliefs are like weeds and, if you want to pull a weed so it never comes back, you need to pull it out by the root. This can involve some tugging and finesse, so the weed doesn't just break off with the root still firmly in the ground. In my exploring and journaling, it obviously wasn't physical tugging I was doing. Instead, the words I wrote involved tugging at my feelings and beliefs. I really wanted to solve this lack of time and money once and for all.

After I gained clarity that I wanted to get to the root of this issue, I wrote these words:

Making money is hard.

Whoa. The reality of those words hit me right in the gut. I realized that particular phrase absolutely *was* my negative belief about money and work. In order to make money, I believed I had to work really hard.

I continued to explore the idea further in my writing because even though my work life was reflecting this "making money is hard" belief, it didn't feel like this belief was truly mine. And if it wasn't my belief, then where did it come from? Where did it originate?

What I discovered from my writing and reflecting was that, as with most negative beliefs, this belief originated when I was a child. Growing up, I witnessed my dad constantly working hard. The only time he was still was when he was napping out of pure and utter exhaustion. He didn't know how to relax. Because he was my role model of what being an adult in the working world was like, I naturally grew up assuming that I had to be as busy as he was and that work and making money would always be hard... and I never questioned that belief. I wasn't even aware of that belief until that very moment, but once I became aware of it, I could see it was always running in the background of my life and business. Like a shadow, it was always there.

It was powerful to realize how this negative belief about money and work first took root and also to become aware of *when this belief first took root in my life.* I could now see how, when I first began working at age 16, I worked as many hours as I could, in addition to going to school. I felt a *compulsion to work hard.* This isn't to say that having a solid work ethic isn't a good thing; working hard at certain times is definitely needed and necessary, especially when starting a business (growing a baby business can be like caring for a newborn!). But *compulsively working* and being unable to relax is very different from having a good work ethic.

Just because working very hard was what I witnessed growing up and what I ended up internalizing when I entered the work world, I did not need to keep living that reality in my own work life — especially when I didn't want to live that reality!

Discovering the origin of my negative belief of "making money is hard" was the beginning step of creating a brand-new reality for how I ran and operated my business. You may also find that doing this inner work around negative beliefs will be powerful for you, too.

After my powerful realization about the root cause of my work and money suffering, I wrote down the new reality I wanted to create for myself going forward: *Making money is easy.*

Now, at first this statement felt like a total lie, and it was. It wasn't true, because that was not at all my experience (yet). And though I had found the root of my negative belief, I had more work to do in order to create a permanent shift. Before I could make a profound shift in my way of thinking, I had to clearly identify how this limiting belief was holding me back in order to create a business and life that embodied my new, positive belief.

Another part of getting to the root of my negative beliefs was realizing I had inherited beliefs from others which were not consistent with what I wanted in my business or my life. We often unconsciously "take on" and model negative beliefs that we learn from our earliest role models — including our parents, older siblings and teachers — and I was no exception.

Common negative beliefs unconsciously picked up in childhood may include:

Life is hard.

Life is hard and then you die.

Wealthy people are miserable.

Relationships are a lot of work.

Strangers are scary.

Most of us just take these negative beliefs for granted, thinking they are ours and rarely wake up from the "belief trance" to realize, *"Wait! Do I really think or feel this way, or is this something I simply picked up from my mom, dad or society as a whole?"*

If left unexamined, these negative beliefs we picked up along the way in childhood can become calcified ways of being, thinking and acting in adulthood. These calcifications become the foundation for how we live our lives, view the world or run our businesses. Without self-reflection, these beliefs lead to us knowing no other way of life; we just assume that's the way we are (or the way our lives or businesses are). These negative beliefs create a self-imposed glass ceiling and then become our comfort zone until one day, without realizing it, we've stepped into a "belief prison" of our own making. And suddenly, we may realize we're not living the life we would like to live. Though this may feel hopeless, all is not lost! Breakdowns often lead to break-throughs.

> **Burnout Recovery Tip:**
> Finding your own negative beliefs is the first step to lasting change. This initial awareness of not living the life you want to live can then pave the way for a whole new way of life—and a new way of running your business.

Rooting Out Your Own Negative Beliefs

To help you discover your own moment of clarity and identify your own latent beliefs that may need to change, I have included four exercises to help you uncover your mental blocks and discover how you may be unintentionally limiting the quality of your life and business. This awareness can help you begin to create necessary changes to recover from burnout and create the life you most desire — to go from merely surviving in your business to truly thriving.

Okay, it's time now for you to start your own unearthing process, to discover what may be preventing you from creating the kind of business and life you want to have, and to get you pointed in the direction of creating what you most desire.

Set aside 60 minutes of undisturbed time to complete the following exercises. If you do not have 60 minutes of quiet time for reflection, focus and writing now, set down the book until you do. You may ultimately decide to jump around through the following chapters based on your current needs, and that's fine, but this part is a crucial starting point, no matter what your situation is now. The remainder of the book will be much more effective and powerful for you *after* you have done these self-reflection exercises.

Tools You'll Need:

- A timer
- Your burnout recovery journal (or computer if you are using an electronic journal) and a pen or pencil, if needed
- A desire to discover and break down the mental blocks contributing to your business burnout

The following exercise is divided into four sections. Close your eyes and take three deep breaths. Open your eyes when you are ready to begin this revealing process. Set your timer for 60 minutes (15 minutes for each section) and begin.

Part One: Your Ideal Balanced Business and Life

Before you begin writing, take a moment to ponder the following questions. Commit to being completely honest with yourself in your answers. Your self-honesty will begin to open the door to more peace and freedom, even if the answers are initially painful.

When you're ready, write your candid, honest responses to these questions in your burnout recovery journal. The more specific you can get, the better. Be sure to let go of your inner perfectionist. Don't spell check, edit or overthink as you write your answers:

What isn't working in my business life? What parts of the business are causing me to feel depleted, stressed and/or anxious?

What changes would need to happen in my business life to go from surviving to thriving; to go from considering divorcing my business to instead falling in love with my business? What would my daily working experience be like and what tasks would I be doing? How many days a week and how many hours a day would I be working?

How will my business improve if I have more mental, physical and emotional energy? What changes will I want to make to my business when I have more creativity and enthusiasm? How would it feel to look forward to going to work? What would I do with my life if I could step away from my business for part of each week or to retire completely?

What isn't working in my personal life? What is causing me stress and strain?

What would my personal life look like on a daily, weekly and monthly basis if I was truly living a life I love?

What specific ways will my personal life improve if I am mentally and emotionally restored instead of burned out? What improvements will I see in my relationships with family and friends? My health? My freedom to explore a new hobby or passion?

Part Two: Roadblocks to Success

Now that you've listed specifics of what a balanced business and personal life look like for you, identify what is preventing your success.

When I had my pet care business, I found myself returning client calls when I did not actually have the time to talk, which then led me to rush through the call. This would sometimes send the unspoken message to my clients that I didn't have time to listen to their needs. It was a small detail, but it had a big, negative impact on my business. Discovering that self-sabotaging behavior and changing when I returned client calls so that I actually had time and space to talk made a big difference in my relationships with my clients, and ultimately, my ability to retain those clients.

Take an honest look at any actions or behaviors you are currently doing (or aren't doing) that may not be serving you or your clients well and are keeping you from nurturing the best relationship with your business and write them here:

- _____
- _____
- _____
- _____
- _____

If you are struggling to identify your sabotaging behaviors, consider these behaviors that are common among many of my pet business coaching clients:

- Spending too much time on Facebook or other social media
- Being unwilling to trust anyone else with the business (not delegating or hiring)
- Failing to set boundaries and enforce policies with clients
- Making unrealistic promises to clients
- Not raising rates for many years

Part Three: Your Unconscious Relationships with Work and Time

Wanting to heal from burnout and actually *making the changes* necessary to experience recovery from burnout are two different things. The next two exercises will help you discover your hidden beliefs about work as you begin your inner process of healing and change.

What do I mean by hidden beliefs about work? Many people believe, as I did early on in my business journey, that business success depends on the constant effort of the business owner. In those first months, and sometimes years, a new business does take a lot of focus and energy to succeed. The problem comes when business owners believe they must continue at the same frantic pace forever. Not only is this false, but it can end up driving many business owners to exhaustion, as well as hurting their business in various ways, which can then cause the business owner to reflexively walk away or sell their business. When you are stretched too thin and don't have the time and space to think objectively about your business, you won't make the best decisions for your business.

With that example in mind, answer the following questions.

Your Beliefs About Money, Work and Stress:

*What subconscious beliefs about **the relationship between money, work and stress** have you inherited from your parents? If you are having a hard time gaining clarity about these inherited negative beliefs, it can be helpful to recall sayings or adages about work or money that you heard growing up that may have contributed to your beliefs and your current burnout.*

- _____
- _____
- _____
- _____
- _____

To help you think of ideas, here are some common adages about money and work you may have heard before:

- "Money doesn't grow on trees."
- "If it sounds too good to be true, it probably is."
- "More money brings more problems."
- "Money is the root of all evil."

Your Beliefs About Time:

*What subconscious beliefs about **time** have you inherited from your parents or picked up throughout your life experience? If you are having a hard time gaining clarity about these inherited negative beliefs, it can be helpful to recall sayings or adages you heard your parents say about time that may have contributed to your burnout.*

- _____
- _____
- _____
- _____
- _____

Here are two sayings about time you may believe without even realizing it:

- "Time is money."
- "Time flies when you're having fun."

Part Four: You Deserve to Recover from Burnout

As I started exploring the mental blocks preventing my own recovery from burnout, I discovered something I wasn't expecting to find: I kept telling myself I would finally relax once I finished a particular project or goal. But then, without fail, there would inevitably be yet another business task to do. I would keep putting off taking time to relax and recharge, telling myself that when I was done with this one more thing, I'd finally take time for myself. Eventually, these "one more things" piled up until it had been years since I'd given myself the gift of relaxation. I call this the "one more thing thing," and I see this a lot in my coaching clients, too. The "one more thing thing" is a damaging pattern when it comes to creating work/life balance. Not only did I deserve rest and relaxation (and I needed it soon if I was ever going to develop a healthy relationship with my business), but you do too, which is probably why you're reading this book.

Finish the following sentence, carefully considering your own beliefs about the recovery you deserve:

I deserve to recover from business burnout because...

- _____
- _____
- _____
- _____
- _____

If you're stumped by this question and can't come up with any answers, you're not alone. It likely means you're suffering from severe business burnout, which can cloud your ability to see why you deserve to be free from this crippling "ailment." Most who were stumped by this question were better able to answer it after reading this book. You likely will be, too!

If you're feeling stuck about why you deserve to recover from business burnout, here are a few reasons that other pet business owners have discovered on their own recovery journeys:

46

- I provide a valuable service for my clients so they can relax, and I deserve relaxation, too.
- Rest and relaxation are not just a want, they are a need.
- We humans, including me, are not wired to work 24/7.
- No one has been on their deathbed and wished they had worked more.

Getting to the root of my negative beliefs and deciding I wanted to create a business that gave me both time and money cracked open my mental block and deep-seated beliefs. I realized I deserved a business that worked for me, instead of the other way around. Once I could see my inner worth and value as an entrepreneur and as an individual, my mindset about so many aspects of my personal and business life changed. Your own moments of clarity can come if you keep your mind open to options you hadn't previously considered possible, much less probable. This chapter may be pushing you to explore ideas, memories, dreams and goals you hadn't even known were there... and that's the point!

See the End Result Before You Begin

"Seeing is believing" may sound trite, but it's a common phrase for a reason. Imagining yourself living the reality of the life and business you want to create is often the first step toward any lasting change. If you cannot truly see yourself in a place of professional success and personal balance, you will not be able to create a new life for yourself. Even if you stumble into success by chance (as I have at various times in my business), you may not be able to sustain that level of success if you cannot envision what your ideal life and business look like. Accidental success cannot be recreated but success on purpose usually can. (Read Jung's quote at the very beginning of this chapter, which highlights how our outer life often reflects our inner state.)

When burned out business owners come to me stuck in a place of negativity and frustration, I ask them what vision they have for their business and personal life. In almost every situation, their worries and fears have started to take the place of their future visioning and goal setting. Often, their previous forward momentum in their business stops and their attention is diverted instead to putting out business fires and solving short-term problems. The more they let fear drive their decision-making, the more that feeds their negativity and frustration (and often the more fires they then have to put out). The good news about this negative spin cycle is that when they recognize it, they can then learn how to stop it.

If you are currently finding yourself in a place of worry and fear or negativity and frustration, whether at work or at home (or both), know that you *can* take control of the narrative, change your long-held beliefs and begin to imagine what it would be like to really achieve your professional and personal goals. This isn't a woo-woo, airy-fairy way of changing your life and business (though some of the exercises contained in the following pages may appear that way because they may be different from anything you've ever tried before); what this book contains is a tangible, solid way to create a *permanent transformation* in your personal and professional life. That transformation has happened in many areas of my life and business, and I've also witnessed it in thousands of pet business owners who have completed the actions in this chapter and the actions contained in the rest of the book during coaching sessions. Though you can certainly sign up for a coaching session with me to guide you through the process, you don't *need* to get a private coaching session with me—it's all outlined here for you. If you follow the steps laid out for you in these pages, you are likely to experience that transformation yourself.

In the last *Action Step* at the end of this chapter, I am going to encourage you to give yourself the gift of 20 minutes to visualize positive personal and business outcomes for yourself. With only 20 minutes to imagine what kind of life and business would be the ultimate reality for you, you will probably already start to begin to generate enthusiasm and ideas for this recovery journey. At the beginning of a coaching session with me, many of my clients already have some idea of what needs to change in order to recover from burnout but aren't sure exactly where to start. As soon as I help them discover what they can actually achieve through a better relationship with their business, they often find the direction they need. Relief is on the way! The following pages will help you get to that place of direction and relief.

Kristin's Story

After I got in touch with my negative belief about "being too old for marriage" that I mentioned earlier, I decided to create an affirmation that would help me begin to rewire neural pathways in my brain when it came to a romantic relationship and to create a new belief that marriage was, in fact, possible for me.

At first, even mentioning the word marriage in my affirmation felt like too big of a leap so I started with the word "relationship" instead of "marriage." The affirmation I created was this: "I am in a happy, healthy, loving relationship with a man who loves and adores me and whom I love and adore." I said this affirmation out loud, several times a day, anywhere I wasn't likely to run into people who would think I was crazy for talking to myself! For me, that usually meant repeating my affirmation while driving or hiking solo in the woods.

Then, after a few weeks, when I'd gotten used to the "relationship" word and began believing that I could in fact be in a great relationship, I inserted the more emotionally-charged (for me) word—"marriage." "I am in a happy, healthy, loving marriage with a man who loves and adores me and whom I love and adore."

I also began saying this affirmation in the first, second and third tense. For example: "I, Kristin Morrison, am in a happy...", "You, Kristin Morrison, are in a happy...", "She, Kristin Morrison, is in a happy..."

There is something incredibly powerful and transformative when we hear ourselves saying affirmations in these three different ways. My example of marriage that I've shared here may not be what *you* want or need right now, especially if you're grappling with exhaustion and stress; however, I encourage you to simply follow the example and create an affirmation today that addresses whatever you most want to create in your life or business. Affirmations are a powerful step to rewire the brain and support the belief that what you want in your work or your life is actually possible and then get you pointed in the right direction to create it.

Burnout Recovery Success Stories

"I've always had a fear of inadequacy. I now focus on what I have to bring to the business that makes it unique instead of focusing on what others are doing that make me feel inadequate. In my case, I have a design background, so I can make our work look professional. I am also good at managing people and making clients feel comfortable."
Stephanie Surjan - Chicago Urban Pets
Chicago, Illinois

"I have had to deal with my negative beliefs and mindset off and on over the years. I've been through numerous health issues (one is forever, one is still pending, the others are in the past) and a bad marriage followed by a rough divorce and the combination of those things led to bankruptcy. It was a very difficult stretch of years that left me very down about myself. (For example, I can't get any clients no matter what I do, I'm poor, my business will never be the same after this pandemic, no one loves me, etc., etc.)

The negative beliefs and repetitive thoughts that I had during that challenging time kept me spinning in a negative mindset. I would have started my pet care business eons ago if my ex-husband had been supportive and positive, and then I just thought I couldn't do anything for the longest time. It took me a long time to get to where I am now. I have my own business and a supportive significant other and have more confidence in myself. It can still be a struggle at times. I have to keep reminding myself what I've been through and the progress I've made and that I can do this.

Anytime I catch myself in a negative mindset, I step back and reset it. I change the wording to positive, 'I GET to do this. I can do ALL things,' and so on. I also change what I'm doing. If I'm sitting there thinking that, I do something else and get moving – change the wording and then literally MOVE AWAY from the negative thoughts. It can be as simple as going to get a drink of water. Standing up straighter. Little things can make a big impact. Scribbling in a journal to get those thoughts out of my head is helpful too if I'm really stuck. Plus, dog walks are fabulous for a reset! Dogs are so good at being present.

I've always known that my mom's beliefs were not mine, but I just pushed it aside thinking I must be wrong if everyone else was telling me the same

thing. After the divorce, it took me a while to discover 'me' again, as I always tried to be what everyone else wanted. At some point I just gave up on myself and did whatever everyone else wanted and expected. Anything else was a battle that wasn't worth it. Or so I thought. Now I know better and after having had time on my own, I refuse to ever be that person again. I like me, and my thoughts and feelings are worth fighting for."
Brienne Carey - BC Pet Care, LLC
Wheaton, Illinois

"A fear of mine has been leaving my business for some much-needed downtime! I am a frequent traveler, especially to third world countries, so I sometimes have limited-to-no phone reception in some rural areas. This has definitely stressed me out knowing that I won't be able to check in with my subcontractors or they won't be able to message me if there is an emergency. However, the past few times I have done this, there have been no dramas at all! I have to learn to completely trust my team and know that they can tackle whatever comes their way."
Natalie Durack - Happy Hounds Dog Walking and Pet Sitting
Gold Coast, Australia

"I went through a period in my life where I really had to work with my negative beliefs. Long story short, my husband left without a word to me or our children. He came and went in our lives for about a year before we officially separated. Financially, I went from a two-income household to a single income and struggled to keep my home and raise my boys. It was a very dark period of time in my life.

The word 'can't' was a mantra for me for many years. 'I can't manage to keep my home for my kids. I can't keep my home. I can't manage the bills.' Second to those thoughts was 'No one will ever love me.'

Luckily, I had some supportive friends who helped me think outside the box. I had 70 acres of land, and a friend told me about conservation easements and also suggested logging. I put my property in an easement with the Commonwealth of Virginia and had selective logging done on the property. These two things greatly helped me with taxes and with becoming more financially stable. I sold the home eventually. All of these things began to make me realize I was stronger and smarter than I had known, and slowly, over the past three years, my life has improved, and I have a renewed purpose.

There were a few behaviors and beliefs I modeled after my parents that I realized weren't really me. My mom was very old-fashioned. She believed in staying at home, marrying well, not working hard. She worked hard around the house, of course, but her 'down time' was soap operas and watching birds. She didn't enjoy doing much of anything outside of the home. The only travel she did was to visit family. She didn't explore, hike, bike, kayak, anything like this. She hated my love of horses and couldn't understand why I'd rather clean a stall on a hot day than sit inside and watch TV. This really rubbed off on me and I am a homebody in a lot of ways. However, I realized she basically lived her life vicariously through television. I decided I didn't want that. I am still very afraid to take risks and really challenge myself sometimes, but I work hard to push through that fear and when I do, I come out on the other side, feeling better about myself, stronger and more knowledgeable.

For example, I'm 59 years old and have not had the opportunity to ride on a regular basis in 24 years but I have a spooky, untrained horse that I am working with and will have a professional train for me. Just so I can hopefully fulfill a dream I've had since I was a small child to do competitive trail riding. Currently, I have physical limitations. That would have been enough to make my mom give up, but not me. I LOVE being outdoors and being active, so I go to docs, physical therapy, whatever, to get over the issues, and WILL eventually ride my horse."
Barbara Link - New River Valley Pet Sitting & Farm Services, LLC Christiansburg, Virginia

"Negative beliefs are a constant struggle for me. Some days are harder than others. In the transition of growing and taking the step out of being the primary pet sitter and dog walker in my company, I struggle letting go. All the fears hold me back. I'm afraid of what the client will think. I'm afraid the pet sitter and dog walker I bring on won't do the job the way I want them to. I'm afraid of how it will make my company look assuming it'll make it look poorly run. I'm afraid of hiring and training the pet sitter or dog walker, bringing them on board with this client, only to have them back out or not be available, etc. I'm also afraid that if I take a step back from doing the actual visits I won't make enough to cover all expenses and my own personal bills. This also ties in with my personal life as it prevents me from having one because I end up working 14-hour days, seven days a

week, leaving little time for myself or any friends and family. I will even look at other companies who seem to be rocking it and give myself so much grief for not doing a good job.

Moving through the fear and acknowledging the negative mindset has helped. Identifying the thoughts that are holding me back and shifting my thoughts to the positive helps. I talk to my support system about these beliefs and I find meditation really helps (though I'm not very consistent with it). Praying is huge! The moment that a negative thought pops in my head, I turn it over to my higher power and ask to be relieved of it. I ask my higher power for the courage to keep moving forward. Taking breaks and treating myself with anything that doesn't relate to this industry helps my brain to reset and get back on that beam."

Michelle Sabia - Paws & Claws Pet Sitting Services
Cave Creek, Arizona, and Litchfield, Connecticut

Action Steps – Root Out Negative Beliefs

Action Step

If you did not already complete the four clarity exercises listed in the chapter, do that now. Start with **Part One: Your Ideal Balanced Business and Life** and work through **Part Four: You Deserve to Recover from Burnout**. These exercises will direct the rest of your recovery journey and help you see what beliefs are holding you back.

Action Step

Using the example I gave at the beginning of the chapter of turning a limiting belief into a positive one, pick a negative belief that you identified during the clarity exercises in this chapter. Then, take that belief and turn it around to create a new, positive expression or affirmation. For example, instead of "I'm too old to get married," I came up with "I am the perfect age to get married." Be aware that this new affirmation will likely feel like a lie at first—mine did! Allow yourself to imagine how this new belief might be true, or even truer than the negative belief.

If creating a new belief is too far a reach for you right now, write your own affirmation statement about your choice — whatever it is you most want to create in your life or business right now. For example, for me, it looked like this: "I choose to believe I have both time *and* money."

Write your own positive belief, statement of choice or positive affirmation. Then, put it somewhere you will see it often, like a bathroom mirror or on your car dashboard, so you will feel inspired to repeat it often throughout your day.

Action Step

Take a moment now to imagine yourself a year from now, relaxed and free of burnout. At the end of the year, you and your business are thriving. Then, set your timer for 20 minutes and open to a new page in your burnout recovery journal. At the top of the page, date it for one year from today. Then, picture yourself one year from now, having made the changes in this book and achieving the life you wrote about in the first *Action Step* above. Allow yourself to think beyond any negative beliefs you still hold and picture the life you are going to build for yourself when you are free from burnout. Write for at least 20 minutes when answering the questions below. Write your answers in present tense, as if what you want to happen has already happened.

How many days a week are you working in your pet business?

What services have you added or dropped in your business?

Have you expanded to any new areas or reduced any service areas?

What tasks are you doing in your business and what tasks have you given to staff to handle?

How many staff members do you employ?

What is your gross (total revenue) and net (after business expenses) income after a year?

Where are you living?

What new activities or hobbies have you added now that have given you a better and more relaxed relationship with your business?

Which personal relationships have improved and how have they improved?

Take a few moments to imagine what could be possible if you take the steps outlined in this book to create a life and business that really work for you.

When the timer rings, make a note on your calendar or set a reminder to review what you wrote in one year. After you've reviewed it a year from now, email me at thrive@SFPBacademy.com. I would love to hear about your progress! Looking back at these pages in a year will help you see how far you have come and what specific changes you made in your business and your life to get there.

Look at

TWO

Put New Beliefs Into Action

How I Brought My New Beliefs to Life— and Created a New Life for Myself

> *"You cannot solve a problem from the same level of consciousness that created it. You must learn to see the world anew."*
>
> –Albert Einstein

As Albert Einstein said so wisely in his quote above, *"You must learn to see the world anew."* When we begin to see the world anew, the old world (or business) as we knew it is gone. In this chapter, I am going to continue my personal story and write about what happened after I uncovered my own negative beliefs and worked to change them. This chapter will lay the groundwork for the important process of making changes that will really stick.

What I'm going to share with you in this chapter may help bridge the gap between your head and your heart when it comes to your business and your life, as well as assist you in getting in touch with *what you don't know that you don't know.*

When we get in touch with "what we don't know that we don't know," many aspects of our business and life may shift in powerful and positive ways.

That is what happened to me.

Finding a Role Model Who Embodied My New Belief

As I worked to transform my own business and life, I searched for a role model who had success as I defined it—specifically, someone with both time and money. However, when I tried thinking of some-one I knew who embodied this "making money is easy" philosophy, someone who had both money and time, someone who wasn't work-ing a large number of hours each week, I couldn't think of anyone.

I was stumped.

I couldn't think of a single business owner I personally knew who was making money in an easy, relaxed and effortless way. The busi-ness owners I knew either had a lot of clients but not a lot of time or they had a lot of time but not a lot of clients.

I hoped that having both time and money could be possible as a business owner, but because I couldn't even think of one person who embodied this reality of a time-rich and financially prosperous busi-ness owner, it didn't seem possible!

However, in my thinking and daydreaming, I continued to explore and imagine what my business and personal life might be like if mak-ing money could truly be easy. I also began discussing the possibility of having both time and money in conversations with my fellow busi-ness-owner friends.

One day, as I was sharing this concept of wanting to have both time and money with a business-owner friend, she said, *"That sounds nice! I wish I had that, too. I know someone who does have both – he's a friend's hus-band – and he's so inspiring to me. He makes money in an easy, relaxed way. In fact, he works 10 hours a week and makes over a million dollars a year!"*

I was so grateful to her for sharing about her friend's husband because even though I (still) have never met this man, even know-ing that a friend of a friend who was a business owner had both time and money was enough for me! Just the thought that someone out there had what I wanted gave me the confidence that I too could make money with ease and without spending all my time focused on work.

One of the most powerful stories I've heard about the power of belief is from the history of competitive runners. You may have heard it too, and if so, I encourage you to read this story in the context of making your own positive beliefs a reality.

In the 1940s and 1950s, runners attempted to be the first to run a mile in less than four minutes. All of the world's top milers could run the mile in just over four minutes, but none had been able to break that four-minute mark. In fact, there was a time when it was believed to be physically impossible because no one had previously done it. However, as the years wore on, runners became convinced that they could shave off those last seconds... but no one had done it yet. Finally, in 1954, Roger Bannister became the first to run a mile in under four minutes (he finished the race at 3:59.4).

And do you know what happened next?

Within weeks, more runners started documenting mile times under four minutes, as well!

Once they knew a mile could be run in under four minutes, they were also able to break the four-minute barrier.

Although each runner was training intensely and determined to run a mile in under four minutes, *until they saw someone else actually break the record*, their belief about what was possible held them back.

I've had similar experiences with my own beliefs, and I'm betting you have, too.

> BELIEF, NOT SKILL, IS WHAT HELD BACK THE WORLD'S FASTEST RUNNERS.

Recalling Situations Where I Experienced My New Belief

After I found my "invisible" role model (my friend's friend), I thought about whether or not I'd ever experienced "making money is easy." I then began looking for examples of the positive belief in action in my own business.

At first, I couldn't see where "making money is easy" had ever shown up in my business. (It's fascinating how when a negative belief is there, like with the example of the four-minute mile, the belief forms a huge block to seeing the opposite as true.) However, simply being willing to explore how it *may* have been possible that making money was easy at least once in my business history helped me recall having a five-minute phone call a few years prior with a client who was going away on vacation for a month. She requested one of her regular pet sitters from my company to care for her animals and as a result of that easy and quick 5-minute phone call I made $1,200 profit!

The lies of "being a successful business owner requires constant effort" and "making money is hard" were beginning to crumble...

Remembering how I'd easily and effortlessly earned that $1,200 opened the door to prior memories of making "easy money" — times I likely would not have remembered or noticed had I not done some inner reflective footwork.

Consciously Working with the New Belief

I began to work with my new belief by writing and speaking the affirmation "making money is easy." I wrote that affirmation on sticky notes and posted them around my house and put one on my dashboard of my car: *Making money is easy.*

And more and more, I began to experience this new belief being true in my life!

Here's the thing, though: Just writing or saying affirmations often doesn't create lasting change. We have to both realize we *deserve* to have what we want and *believe* that it is possible in order to have what we want. We don't have to know *how* it's going to happen; we just have to believe that it can and likely will happen. And I don't mean thinking or saying "I deserve money" in an entitled, snobby way. Not at all. I mean experiencing the feeling of deserving money in the same way that every child deserves love.

For me, beginning to believe this affirmation was possible through seeing examples in my own life and in the lives of others (even if I'd never met them!), as well as truly understanding that it was okay to make money and that I deserved money — all of this had to be done in tandem.

All of this newfound awareness (some might call the inner belief work I did navel-gazing; I call it *revelatory and game-changing*), wasn't just about me simply sitting on my laurels wishing for it to be true as I said my affirmation. Yes, it involved me saying and writing this affirmation, but it also required me to *internalize* this new belief. That internalization could only happen with my deserving and believing it was possible. To begin to truly experience this new, positive belief in my life, I needed to take solid actions that supported my new positive belief.

In the next chapter, I will walk you through the solid actions I took — the process of connecting and checking in with your own business through a powerful process called "active imagination."

Kristin's Story

Many years ago, I began writing goals for myself in the form of affirmations. At the start of every new year, I would think about what I most wanted to achieve. I then wrote those "affirmation goals" and taped them to my bathroom mirror where I would see them every day. When friends would come over, they would see my goals on the mirror, as well. They often commented on them; some were inspired to create their own affirmations and others would tease me a bit about them.

One friend named Daniel came over one day and saw them on my mirror and he started laughing. He could barely talk he was laughing so hard, but he managed to say, "So you think writing these down is really going to help you?!" I recall feeling embarrassed at the time (this was about 20 years ago). In fact, his reaction even caused me to want to remove the affirmations from my only bathroom mirror in my house, but my desire to achieve those things I had written was stronger than my embarrassment. And that mirror was something I knew I'd look at every day, so I decided to keep them there.

Daniel and I lost touch a couple of years after that.

Fast forward to two years ago (about 18 years from the time he'd laughed at my affirmations). Daniel found me on Facebook and we reconnected there. In a message he wrote me this:

"Kristin, I don't know if you remember but I laughed at your affirmations many years ago. I thought it was ridiculous. Well, I'm looking at your life: married to a great guy, owner of a successful business, etc. All the things you wrote down came true! They came true! I'm both stunned and happy for you. I'm sorry I laughed at you that day. I actually wish I'd been doing this all along in my life, because I certainly don't have the kind of life I want in this moment. I think I'm going to try writing affirmations and putting them on my bathroom mirror!"

While I did not post my affirmations to impress or guide anyone else, I found that others, like Daniel, did notice. After I became someone who was intentional, motivated and successful at achieving my goals, I became someone that others wanted to emulate. You may find the same is true for you, too.

Burnout Recovery Success Stories

"Even though I have 14 diplomas in the Animal Care sector that I achieved high grades in and I have attended many other courses to make sure that I am knowledgeable in my field and can provide a great service, I still sometimes feel that my best isn't good enough. This was made more challenging during the COVID-19 lockdown because I am not very good with computers and it took me a long time to develop the skills that I needed to help clients – I certainly didn't feel that I was good enough and was worried about all the people I was letting down because of this. I kept hearing myself say 'I can't do this,' I kept thinking I wasn't good enough and I had days and nights where this was all I could think about and I felt like a complete failure.

To change my mindset, I looked back at what I have already achieved and started to study. I completed many new courses and enrolled for my advanced diploma in animal behavior, which gave me something positive to focus on. I also tried to focus on all of the wonderful feedback that I was getting from clients and how I can shape my future and not be so hard on myself!"

Kirsty Everard – Kirsty's Paws
Bournemouth, United Kingdom

"I struggle with anxiety and depression, so it is easy for me to get wrapped up in negative thinking. Some negative beliefs and repetitive thoughts that kept me spinning in a negative mindset were: 'My business will close,' 'I'll lose all my clients,' 'No one will want to work with me' and 'I'll lose everything I've worked for.'

Over time, I have been able to change those negative beliefs in order to create a different and more positive mindset. Therapy has helped me immensely in my tendency to worry about personal and business matters. Specifically, I've learned to focus on the facts and focus on things I can control. For example: Fact – I have a loyal client base that has proven to be very supportive. Fact – There are plenty of people who need pet care and training. Even if I lose a few clients for one reason or another, I will gain the right clients elsewhere. Things I can control when it comes to my business – Spending time in

business support groups, learning more about marketing and professional development."
Ashley Farren – Ashley's Animal Academy, LLC
Downingtown, Pennsylvania

Action Steps – Put New Beliefs Into Action

Action Step

Using the example from this chapter of runners breaking the four-minute mile record, think about experiences in your own life. When is a time that you have succeeded after building a new belief? Write about this experience (or, if you have many, make a list) in your burnout recovery journal. As I mentioned in the chapter, simply being willing to explore how an ideal *may* have been achieved can help you recall when it *did*.

For me, remembering how I'd easily and effortlessly earned money one specific time then opened the door to prior memories of making "easy money." This memory or list will hopefully do the same for you and your new, positive beliefs.

Action Step

Work on your new, positive beliefs by creating affirmations for yourself. In your burnout recovery journal, write at least one affirmation that embodies your new belief(s). Then, write the affirmation on sticky notes or note cards and post them around your house and in your car. Every time you see the note, read and say your affirmation to internalize your new belief.

THREE

Let Active Imagination Guide Your Burnout Recovery

The Power of Imagery and Active Imagination

"When solving problems, dig at the roots instead of just hacking at the leaves."

–Anthony J. D'Angelo

If you're like many of the business owners I know and work with, you've perhaps tried to "cure" your business burnout before. Long before you picked up this book, you probably recognized that something significant needed to change in order to recover from burnout and prevent it from ever returning — perhaps you realized you needed more self-care, more sleep or better boundaries with clients. And yet, here you are... burned out and looking for a solution that could actually work. If your methods had worked, you probably wouldn't be reading this book, correct? Given that, you really have nothing to lose by simply *trying* what I will be encouraging you to do in this chapter and in the rest of the book.

I invite you to open that mind of yours, that same intelligent, courageous mind that started your business from a thought and turned it into a thing. That same powerful mind that has perhaps grown your business into something far bigger and more magnificent (and perhaps more challenging) than you could have ever imagined when you first had the thought to start a business.

However, that same mind of yours, as brilliant and intelligent as it is, could be getting in the way here, and *could actually be one of the biggest factors that's causing your burnout.*

If your current structure (in other words, your business) isn't working, and if whatever prior way you've attempted to fix that structure hasn't worked, then you'll want to clear out the debris that's not working and build a new foundation from which to create something new. You can't build on an old foundation. You have to first dismantle that old foundation, and only then can you build the structure (or business) of your dreams.

Fortunately, you will not need to start your business from scratch; I will give you the tools you need to transform your existing business. This chapter is the *bulldozer and the bedrock* from which to build the business that you can now only just imagine. The kind of business that no longer runs you, but that you skillfully run in an empowered, confident way.

Before we dive into this though, you have to know, this chapter is *edgy.*

How is it edgy? Well, in the following pages, I'm going to be encouraging you to explore yourself, your business and your life in ways you've perhaps never before explored, nor ever even thought to explore. The methods I'm suggesting may seem "out there," but they have helped me and many of my coaching clients realize what is truly needed to make permanent changes that actually last when it comes to burnout.

Though it may seem counterintuitive to explore the inner realm first rather than the outer aspects of your business when it comes to curing your work stress, this inner realm is where your real burnout recovery starts.

The exercises contained in this chapter have worked wonders for me, which is why I included this information here.

These edgy exercises have also worked for many of my open-minded, willing and courageous coaching clients who were so burned out and weary that they were ready to try anything. This included being open to some very unusual methods I invited them to explore in their coaching sessions in order to get to the root of what was causing their burnout—burnout that persisted no matter what remedies they'd previously tried.

I first learned about the process I'll be sharing in this chapter when I read a book by the Swiss psychoanalyst Carl Jung. In his book, Jung wrote how he would work with patients who had tried everything they could think of to solve their particular deeply-rooted problems — problems like addiction to alcohol or drugs, relationship problems, money challenges and other issues. His patients were often quite desperate for a solution when they contacted him for help, usually because they'd previously tried many other methods to get relief but with no success. Jung did a process with them that previously he'd only done with himself. He called this process "active imagination," and it worked wonders for many of his patients!

I was fascinated by what I read about this process and, after learning more about active imagination, I decided to try it with my ever-present business burnout that I couldn't seem to shake, no matter how many tangible changes I had made in my business. You'll read about my active imagination experience, as well as some of my coaching clients' experiences, in the following pages.

Jungian Imagery and Dream Incubation

Before I guide you through the active imagination exercises, it may be helpful to understand how this first came to be for Carl Jung. One area that interested Jung in his research was how and why we dream at night. He used dreams in his own self-analysis and worked to understand if and how he could use his dreams to cure his own internal conflicts. When Jung was asked to describe his research and work, he said, "...I learned how helpful it can be, from the therapeutic point of view, to find the particular images which lie behind emotions."

I have a friend who is a dream researcher, and she has shared with me the many benefits of "dream incubation" and because of that, I have learned to keep a dream journal near my bed and to write down specific questions in my journal in a concise and clear way before going to sleep. Before falling asleep, she instructed me to ask the specific question I wanted an answer to a few times so that it would be in mind while I fell asleep.

The first time I used this dream technique, I was in the beginning stages of starting my pet care business. Deciding what to name it had kept me stuck. Until I decided upon a business name, I couldn't get a business license, a business bank account, or market my business. I felt really frustrated and at a loss on how to move forward to come up with the right business name.

One night, after weeks of struggling with what to name my business, I recalled my dream researcher's instruction about dream incubation, and I decided to try it. I wrote this question in the journal I kept near the bed: *What should I name my business?* and asked myself that question a number of times as I went to sleep. The first few nights of asking that question before sleep, nothing happened; I couldn't even remember any dreams. It was disappointing! I told my dream researcher friend about it and she encouraged me to keep doing it until an answer came. And sure enough, within a few days after that, I had a dream that I was standing beside my car and I was completely surrounded by happy pet owners with dogs, cats, horses and even some pet owners holding fishbowls with fish swimming around! In my dream, my car had the name "WOOF! Pet Sitting and Dog Walking Service" written across the side of it.

The morning after I woke up from that dream, I went to my local city hall and applied for a business license for "WOOF! Pet Sitting and Dog Walking Service." This is just one example of the power of dream incubation, but it hopefully gives you an idea of how your subconscious and your nighttime dreams can help you in more specific ways than you might have thought if you will only give them the chance to help!

Since the time of his dream research, the concepts Jung suggested have inspired further research by other experts on everything from how your dreams can answer questions that you can't seem to find an answer to, to using other methods (like my business name example), all the way to how to tap into your inner emotions and discomfort and bring them to the forefront where you can address them. This technique Jung had of interacting with his own subconscious imagery became known as "active imagination."

Connecting and Cultivating a Relationship with the Soul of My Business

I used Jung's powerful process of active imagination when I took an unusual step in my burnout recovery to "check in" with my business the way I would with my husband, a family member or a beloved friend. If this sounds strange to you, I understand, but think about it this way: You spend a lot of time with your business and whether you like it or not, you do have a relationship with your business (whether it's a good, bad or a "meh" relationship, only you can know). Because of the relationship between you and your business, it's important that you both are on the same page as far as what's happening and the direction you both are going.

The first time I checked in with my business was many years ago and, though it seemed odd for me to connect with my business in that way, I'm glad I did because it completely altered the course of my business. It's also one of the primary reasons this book exists.

I wanted to figure out why I was experiencing so much stress and strain in my business and, though I had never read anything in Jung's writing about active imagination working with businesses, I felt like I had nothing to lose by trying. I first did a short meditation to quiet my mind. Then, when I felt calm, I "called my business in" and invited it to sit in front of me. (If this is sounding strange to you, we're definitely now at the edgy part that I mentioned earlier!)

It took a couple of minutes to even see anything in my mind's eye, but then I saw a huge and towering dog who looked like McGruff the Crime Dog. Remember McGruff?

My initial instinct was to laugh when I saw my business appear like that character, but thankfully, I remembered the stern advice from Jung for those who practiced active imagination: *honor and respect whatever image shows up.* According to Jung, the first image you see is likely "it," so it's important to accept that first image, no matter how silly or strange it may seem, and let it show you and tell you what it wants to reveal.

So, there is McGruff, and I can see a little version of me holding tightly onto his leg.

After a moment, McGruff said to me, *"I am meant to be big — a lot bigger than I am now. You need to let me grow. You are holding on so tight. You need to let go in order for me to grow."*

I said to my business, *"I do want to let go."*

"Then do it," my business (McGruff) said firmly. *"Let go of your fear and take action."*

Through this simple conversation and others I had with my business, I realized I was afraid to do what needed to be done, which was to hire office help so I could begin to step away from the business. I very much needed to hire a manager in my business in order to begin to let go, but I was afraid to do that because I'd had a very painful experience with a manager a few years earlier.

What happened years ago was this: I had hired a manager I trusted and who had become more like a dear friend than a staff member. In the end though, she betrayed me by taking a number of my clients when she started her own business. She did this with ultimately disastrous results for the clients she took. Even though most of my clients came running back to me because they had a bad experience with her, her betrayal had deeply affected me and caused me to be afraid to ever release control to an office person again. However, if I wanted both time and money like I told myself I did, I would have to take the guidance McGruff had given me and move through my fear and hire a manager.

That conversation with my business as my guide inspired me to step through my fear and hire a loyal manager who ended up working for me four days a week so I could then enjoy a three-day workweek.

Even with all this inner and outer growth that I experienced in my business as I stepped away from working in the business full time, there's always a new edge and new opportunities for growth. A couple of years later, my next growth edge came in the form of a friend sharing with me that she was going on a two-month backpacking trip abroad. I was unexpectedly broadsided by a wave of jealousy — I yearned to go on an extended trip too!

> **Burnout Recovery Tip**
> Strong emotions, such as jealousy and resentment, can often point to an unmet need or want. Listen to those emotions and let them tell you what you need.

I know when I experience the uncomfortable emotion of jealousy, it's often a huge clue to a need or strong desire I have that isn't yet fulfilled in my life. If I only pay attention to the jealousy, then I'm stuck in a miserable, swirling vortex of hopelessness and envy; but if I use the jealousy as a compass, it can become an important indicator that can cause me to *explore* how to fulfill that currently unmet need.

But when I was broadsided by that unexpected jealousy over my friend's extended trip, I had no idea how to fulfill that need of extended travel! Even though I was now only working three days a week and had a manager I trusted, I couldn't imagine traveling abroad for months at a time while my business ran under her care.

I'd initially created my business to support one of my top values (freedom), but I still felt somewhat enslaved by my business even though I was only working three days a week. The thought of traveling for more than a week or two seemed impossible. But my desire to travel for a long period of time would not go away, so I decided once again to walk through my fear to create the life I wanted.

I wanted to ask my manager if she would manage the business for me, but again my old friend fear popped up — what if she said no? Then there would be no way (at least in my mind) for me to travel. Or, what if she said yes but didn't do a good job and I came home to a business that was no longer running properly or had crashed and burned?

But I decided to conquer my fear! I decided to simply ask for what I wanted and see what happened. So, that's what I did. To keep myself accountable (and to get extra support), I "bookended" that manager conversation with a friend before I called my manager. Bookending is something I've learned to do when I have a difficult task I need to tackle. I highly recommend it!

I called my friend and said, *"I'm scared that, when I ask my manager if she will manage my business for a few months while I travel, that she will say no, and my dream of extended travel will die with her saying no."*

She said to me, *"I understand you're afraid. If you don't ask, the answer is no. If you do ask, she may actually say yes. Have this conversation even though you're afraid."*

In the end, I did ask if she would manage my business while I took a long trip out of the country. And she said yes! The next day I bought a non-refundable ticket. Over the course of my subsequent three-month trip, I made more money *not working* than I'd ever made working in my business.

Read that again to let it sink in.

I made more money not working than I had while working.

That's right.

Making money truly was easy.

So easy that I made money while I was eating mangoes in Bali and skinny dipping in jungle pools and immersing myself in an Ayurvedic cleanse in India.

How did I do it?

Well, it started with that manager call and her saying yes. But what followed to make "easy money" was that I subleased my home in the United States while I lived abroad. Also, I often stayed in countries where the cost of living was extremely low. My business continued to make money while I was away. I paid my manager a percentage of money earned for profit sharing and because of this, she was highly motivated to grow the business and run it well while I was away.

While on my three-month trip, I had both time and money.

And after experiencing it so fully, making money became a no-brainer at that point. When you begin to see your new belief reflected around you in the life you're living, you can't ever go back to that old way of viewing the world!

So I came back from that trip and then left a few months later for another extended trip—this time for eight months!

Owning a pet business has brought about some of my greatest challenges but, like with life, those challenges are always opportunities for growth, even though they often don't feel like that when we first experience them.

The process of getting clear about my negative belief, pulling the root, finding a role model, having active imagination conversations with my business and asking it for guidance all created an open door for me to kick my burnout to the curb.

> WHEN YOU BEGIN TO SEE YOUR NEW BELIEF REFLECTED AROUND YOU IN THE LIFE YOU'RE LIVING, YOU CAN'T EVER GO BACK TO YOUR OLD WAY OF VIEWING THE WORLD!

I went from working seven days a week to working three days a week. I went from desiring to travel and feeling green with envy to getting on a plane and zipping off to exotic parts of the world.

I became the visionary captain at the helm of my business "ship," instead of a worker in the belly of the ship, and I ended up making more money and having more time than I'd previously made or enjoyed without doing any more work.

Leading My Clients Through Active Imagination Experiences

Many of my coaching clients I've guided through active imagination have had miraculous, life-altering and profound business experiences and personal changes. I can't guarantee that will happen for you, but if there's even a slight possibility that you could have a life-changing experience when it comes to experiencing relief from burnout, stress and lack of a personal life, it's at least worth a try, right?

The coaching clients I've worked with in this process were led on a guided active imagination journey by me in private coaching sessions. Just as you may be stepping out of your comfort zone by reading this chapter and doing the exercises at the end, I too stepped out of my comfort zone the first time I offered to work with one of my coaching clients in this way.

I knew active imagination had worked wonders for me in my own business and in my life (I use this process on so many areas of my life now), but could it work with my coaching clients in a phone session?

The first time I offered to work with a pet business owner in this way, my client was on the East Coast and I was on the West Coast. She was a longtime client I'd worked with regularly once or twice a month for a few years. Through the many years of owning her pet business, she'd experienced a lot of positive rewards from her business: company growth, she'd become renowned as a pet expert in her local community and had created an abundance of profit. In spite of all these rewards, she was still struggling with overworking and the lack of a personal life. She was lonely and exhausted; her work was her entire life and she wanted that to change.

After helping her start and grow her business, I observed that she was now experiencing the stress of success. I pulled out many items from my coaching toolbox in order to help her run her business rather than letting it run her. Each time, she'd get some occasional relief from her burnout, but it wouldn't stick.

I took a deep breath and went out on a limb. I offered to lead her on a guided active imagination meditation to see what advice her business might give about how to solve her burnout issue.

She was quiet for a few very long moments and then she gamely said, *"Okay, let's do it."*

So, in that moment, I stepped out of my comfort zone and so did she and we jumped down the active imagination abyss together.

In that active imagination session, she called her business in and received very specific guidance and advice on how to move forward with her pet sitting and dog training business. She also had some profound personal revelations as a result of that session, including what a bully and ruthless taskmaster she'd been to herself all these years of business ownership and how that bully part of her would never allow her to relax, no matter how many positive changes she made in her business.

After that, her business was never the same; nor was my coaching practice.

From that moment on, I have offered active imagination as a coaching option for my clients, but only for those who meet two criteria: (1) I think they are open-minded enough to participate in this very unusual type of coaching session, and (2) I can see that active imagination may be what is most needed for them to get to the next level in their business or personal life. I can't tell where each reader (you) fits within those criteria, so it will be up to you to decide if you are ready to courageously step outside of your comfort zone by trying something new and really committing to this experience.

I've coached thousands of pet business owners for over twenty years. Of those clients, I have only suggested this active imagination process to a quarter of my client base. I know most would *not* be open to it, and if so, I never mention it as an option! Those I never mention it to clearly only want solid, tangible action steps from me to get them from point A to point B in their business. And that's fine! It takes all kinds of people to make this world go around, and I enjoy working with all types of business owners, including the left brainers who aren't interested or able to swing into their right brain and try something new and edgy like active imagination.

The tangible, solid, left-brain actions are very important in business, which is why you'll see that a number of chapters in this book are devoted to left-brain solutions for business burnout. That left brain is crucial when it comes to starting and growing a business. But sometimes, no matter how many tangible, left-brain actions are done, using the left brain to solve deep-rooted problems doesn't always work. Sometimes, no matter how many tangible actions we've taken, we'll end up right where we started within a few weeks or months if we haven't dealt with the root cause of why something continues to occur (like ongoing stress and burnout). The reason we may keep circling back to the same overwhelm may be because we haven't dealt with the root cause; we've only dealt with the symptom. And when we don't deal with root causes, symptoms often come back. (Refer back to Chapter One for more guidance on getting to the root of your limiting beliefs.) That's why self-care, though absolutely necessary on an ongoing basis, may only temporarily ease burnout unless it is combined with another, deeper solution. Self-care often addresses the symptom, not the root cause. Active imagination is one way to further identify and deal with the root cause you identified in Chapter One, which is why I'm inviting you to step outside of your left-brained comfort zone and into brand-new territory here.

As I've described in this chapter, I know from personal experience that lasting change will likely not happen — in your business or in your life — until your subconscious mind is in sync with both your conscious mind and your actions. Because these experiences that relied on my imagination and subconscious — instead of tangible, actionable lists of work to do — were so helpful and clarifying for me, I am including a condensed version here for you.

Putting Active Imagination to Work

Active imagination has been described as being half asleep or dreaming while you are awake. Jungian imagery encourages you to allow your subconscious to tell you what you need to know about yourself (and possibly reveal what you might not even know you know!). In this section, I will give you steps to tap into that imagery yourself, but you probably won't feel like you're half asleep or dreaming. All you need to do is open up your mind to images or symbols you might otherwise ignore when you try active imagination. This visualization can allow you to change your inner beliefs first, which then can more easily pave the way for outer change to happen (for example, having more time and money). Those inner adjustments will enable the changes you make to your actions to be more enduring.

When I guide my coaching clients through an active imagination session, I first instruct them to get comfortable in their chair and then inhale and exhale deeply in order to relax. This relaxation time helps them get prepared and ready to hear, see and discover the answers from within.

Some of my coaching clients found that doing active imagination on their own, without me guiding them, was a lot more challenging than doing it with me guiding them. Even though it was more difficult doing it on their own, through practice, they were eventually able to do it themselves and have similar results as they had in their sessions with me.

Then there were others who simply couldn't do active imagination without me (or someone else) guiding them. Then there were still others who could quickly and easily dive into their own "imaginal realms" after having only one guided session with me or by simply reading about or hearing me share about this process. You may be able to do active imagination simply by reading about it in this chapter and then doing it on your own. You won't know until you try, so definitely make a commitment to yourself to at least try this after you've read this chapter in full.

If you follow the steps I outline and keep an open mind and heart, you may experience results too. And if not, contact me for a coaching session, and I'll guide you on an active imagination journey that may open up a whole new world of self-discovery in your life or business (or both).

The best part about what I'll be sharing here about active imagination is that it can be used for *nearly anything* you're struggling with that you haven't been able to fix on your own or with the help of someone else, no matter what you've tried in the past.

Your Own Active Imagination Experience

You will need a full two hours of undisturbed time to work through all of the activities below. If you need to break this up into smaller chunks of available time, that's fine, just give yourself at least a few extra minutes at the beginning of each segment to get back into the mindset you were in when you had to step away.

Pick a quiet place where you won't be disturbed. If you don't have a quiet environment, noise cancelling headphones or earplugs will be your best friend for this experience! I definitely recommend you find a room where you can be alone. You may feel vulnerable as you explore your inner emotions—if you are also worried about someone walking in during the activity, you will probably find it hard to fully relax.

Also, it's important to know that your active imagination experience can feel like a dream when it's over. Right after it's over, the imagery may be in your awareness and clear as day. But then a few minutes pass, and the memories of what you've experienced may be harder to remember and hold in your mind, like wispy clouds. Though simply having the experience is often enough without having to keep a written record of what happened and what was said, if you'd like to remember your experience in detail, I recommend having a pen and journal nearby to write down your experience to refer back to later.

If you do choose to write down your impressions, only do so after you've had your full experience. Resist the urge to write about your experience while it's happening. Stopping your active imagination to record impressions would be like trying to drive with your foot on the gas and the brake at the same time. Stay for the whole active imagination experience and/or conversation until it's completely finished. When it's fully complete, you can then freely write about your experience.

If you'd like to do an active imagination exercise to connect to your business (and if you're experiencing burnout, I recommend that as a good place to start), first think about the most important question you'd like to ask your business. (See #5 in the coming pages to find out more about possible questions to ask.) Once you've chosen a question, prepare to ask that specific question when you check in with your own business.

It's important to know that stillness in both your body and mind is important as you begin. Why? Consider how you would be with a wild animal if you wanted it to approach you. You wouldn't go crashing through the woods trying to catch it. You would sit quietly and let it come to you. Calling the soul of your business in is like that too.

Think of the soul of your business as a wild animal. Wild animals come to us on their own terms. Let your business come to you in its time.

Also, trust that whatever shows up and what is said is the right thing. I've found the language of my soul speaks in symbols, images and sometimes words. You may see and "hear" nothing, or you may come away with valuable informational gold bars or nuggets related to your particular situation. Trust yourself, trust what emerges and what is said and most importantly, trust the process.

1. **Set the stage for a sacred conversation.** Close your eyes and clear your mind. Take a few deep breaths. Meditate or simply be quiet for five minutes. Come to a place within yourself of stillness and calm.

2. **Take a few more deep breaths and call in your business or a pressing issue on your mind.** "I now call you in, [your business name/the issue at hand]."

3. **Be patient for its emergence in its own time and be open and accepting with whatever form, shape or color your business takes when it appears.** Trust that whatever first shows up is the right image. Often, it's what we least expect or we're most surprised by. Don't judge what image shows up or how your business reveals itself to you. Whatever shows up may seem ridiculous or strange. What shows up could be a nebulous blob that has absolutely no form. It's all good. Regardless of what form your business or issue emerges as, be respectful, open and willing; welcome it the way you would welcome a beloved family member who is at your front door. Remember the advice from Jung: *to honor and respect whatever shows up.* Your "wild animal" is here. Thank it. Thank it for showing up in whatever form it has revealed itself to you. It has graced you with its presence. Also be aware that image may change at some point during your conversation with it, and if so, let it change.

4. **Be a welcoming, quiet, receptive presence. Give it time and space to speak to you.** Your instinct may be to want to immediately ask it questions. Resist that instinct. You can ask questions later. When it first arrives, give it space and time to

speak when it is ready. It may be helpful to think of what is now in front of you as a guest who has finally arrived after a long and perhaps grueling journey.

5. **If, after a while, your honored guest doesn't initiate the conversation, begin the conversation by asking it a short, open-ended question.** Ask something like, "What do you have to tell me?" or "What guidance do you have to give me about _____ [one issue you are struggling with in your business or your life]?" Keep your question open-ended (no "yes or no" questions) and keep your question to one short sentence.

6. **After you've asked your question, listen.** Zip up that mouth of yours and listen more deeply than perhaps you've ever listened in your life. It may take a while for what's in front of you to speak, so you'll want to be patient. Or it may answer immediately like it's been waiting all its life to communicate with you! Regardless, be open to whatever response you receive and trust the very first response from it. Just like you want to fully accept what form has shown up in front of you, you want to also accept what is being said. You may "hear" or see the response in your mind's eye, or another way entirely. Trust the process.

7. **After the initial question and response, it may feel right to ask another open-ended question.** Trust that you'll know what to ask and when. The most important thing is to truly hear what is being said and, just let what wants to happen, happen. Often, the more open you are to the experience, the better and more illuminating the experience will be.

8. **When it feels right to end the conversation, thank it for revealing itself to you and for sharing its wisdom with you, or whatever else you want to say.**

9. **Get your journal out and write and/or draw your experience and the information you received.**

With these experiences, you will be able to gain more clarity in curing your burnout and restoring balance to your business and life.

Kristin's Story

A few years ago, I had a client who was grappling with compulsive overworking and was completely exhausted. For some unknown reason, she just could not allow herself to relax, no matter what she tried. I offered to do an active imagination session with her to see if that could help her shift out of this, and she told me she was willing to try anything.

She wanted to talk to the part of herself that was a compulsive worker, so in her mind's eye, she called that part of herself into the room. Nothing showed up for a while, and she wondered if perhaps it wasn't working. I encouraged patience and told her to let what wanted to show up to do so in its time, not hers. She took some deep breaths and waited. Before long, she saw this woman with a riding crop. The woman had her hair in a tight bun, her clothes were tight, everything about this woman was constricted, including her lips, which were pursed.

My client had a deep and profound conversation with this woman, this up-until-now buried part of herself. Through their talk, they were able to come to a resolution that the woman with the riding crop would stop forcing my client to work faster, harder, more, and in return, my coaching client would give the riding crop woman something she desperately wanted — validation for all she'd helped my client accomplish. She had been the primary motivator and driving force for my client's success. Through her urging, my client had accomplished and achieved great things in her business and personal life. The woman in her mind's eye wanted to be acknowledged for her part in what my client had created. When my client gave her that, she eased up on the pushing.

Even after this exercise, the woman with the riding crop would occasionally become a relentless pusher, and my client would find herself not being able to relax again. That would be a sign that she needed to stop, take a deep breath, connect to that inner part of herself and say, "Thank you!" to the part that was helping her accomplish great things.

Burnout Recovery Success Stories

"Some of the most powerful experiences I had while working with Kristin were the active imagination experiences. During one coaching session with her, I was extremely burned out with work and other things going on in life, but I wasn't sure what I really needed.

While doing an active imagination with Kristin I was able to get in touch with some of my unconscious feelings and thoughts. I was able to look at and address the need I had by talking with a part of myself that I had been ignoring.

I know it sounds a little weird, but it was powerful and helped me make some adjustments in my life that were really beneficial to my business and my relationships in the long run.

In another session with Kristin, I remember the active imagination taking me to a deep pit where I was chained down and unable to break free. It took some time exploring, but by the end of the session, it became clear what was subconsciously holding me back. I was able to look at some false beliefs I had been holding onto that I didn't even realize I had.

Kristin helped me create some power affirmations and encouraged me to move beyond the false beliefs by repeating the new affirmations daily. The shifts in thinking helped me overcome some obstacles I had been facing in my business and move to the next level."

Heather Gibson – Elevated Cattery
Salt Lake City, Utah

Action Steps – Let Active Imagination Guide Your Burnout Recovery

Action Step

If you did not already complete the steps listed in the "Your Own Active Imagination Experience" section of this chapter, do so now. Start with "Set the Stage for a Sacred Conversation" and continue through the end of the section. Although this may be outside of your comfort zone, this experience has the potential to guide your burnout recovery journey in a personal and targeted way.

Action Step

Active imagination experiences are like dreams in some ways. If not written down, the details of your experience are likely to fade and be harder to remember over time. Take 15 minutes (or as long as you need) to record your experience in your burnout recovery journal. Be sure to include what you saw, felt or heard and any ideas you had during the experience. This journal entry will be your record and will allow you to partially relive the experience even as you forget the details over time.

Part Two

Put Balance Into Your Business

*"No matter how much I get done or is left undone,
at the end of the day, I am enough."*

–Brené Brown

FOUR

Take the "Busy" Out of Your Business

Create Meaningful Progress by Letting Go of Overdoing

"Stop the glorification of busy."

–Guy Kawasaki

So far in this book, you have focused on the inner aspects of your burnout and mindset. You've stretched your comfort zone (yay, you!) and really dug into the root causes of your burnout. Now it is time to start looking at the specific practices in your business that are contributing to your burnout (and what to do about them). For many pet business owners, one of the main factors adding to burnout is simply being too busy.

In the last few years, being productive has become a badge of honor. In many circles, saying, "I'm so busy" is said as often as "Hello" or "What do you do for work?" Society and the busyness of those around us have conditioned us to believe that having a full schedule and running from one task to another means we're vitally productive, valuable and important. For some, working a lot can be an addiction and a compelling way not to feel emotions they'd rather ignore. For others, being constantly busy is a way to prove their self-worth. This may seem like an exaggeration, but think about it: if you are really busy and your plans suddenly fall through, are you left feeling happy about your open schedule or unmoored and directionless? For many who are suffering from burnout and are overcommitted and overworked, it's the latter.

I have also heard many of my coaching clients share that they are running from task to task so frantically that even if they have a spare hour, they have no idea what to do first. These pet business owners are so busy rushing through the many tasks they need to check off their to-do lists each day that they don't have time to do the hard, but important, work of self-reflection and change.

As I mentioned in my story at the beginning of the book, there was a time that I took great pride in how busy I was. Being busy made me feel successful and important. And yet, that same busyness was draining my life force, preventing me from having a rich personal life, meaningful relationships and draining the joy out of running my business. Before you can create your own transformation and escape your burnout, you will need to take an honest look at the "busy" in your life and in your business.

Give Your Business Space to Breathe

Some businesses fail because they do not have enough clients and/or do not make a profit, but many profitable businesses also fail when the owner reaches a breaking point and chooses to simply close the doors and walk away or sell the business. The same thing almost happened to me before I radically changed the way I did business.

In the coming chapters, you will find suggestions and help for how to set up your business to be automated (to operate without you as much as possible), but that automation starts with a willingness to let go of at least *some* of the control of your business, which is often not an easy step for those who are self-employed. Letting go is as much a mental struggle as it is a practical one. Each time you take an intentional step toward giving your business space to operate without you will be another profound opportunity to reinforce a new mental shift. You and your business both need you to recognize that you will both be better off if you stop insisting on being involved in every single business task. In the first chapter of this book, I walked you through the beginning steps to make that mental shift. In this chapter, I will show you specific ways to create that separation.

LETTING GO OF CONTROL IS AS MUCH A MENTAL STRUGGLE AS IT IS A PRACTICAL ONE.

As I mentioned earlier, businesses are relationships. Just like you need a mix of autonomy and togetherness with your spouse or significant other, your business needs a combination of closeness and separation with you in order to fully thrive. A healthy balance of autonomy and connection is the best way to run your company — for you and for the business.

The first step to giving your business space to breathe is to realize your business is separate from you. Though you run it, your business is not you. Even though it may feel at times like it's who you are and part of your identity, it's actually not. Your business is something you've created (or purchased).

The next step is to let go of control and learn to delegate. You'll read more about that in detail in Chapter Eight. You can start preparing now to let go of control and delegate by setting up parts of your business to function automatically. That automation may take more effort initially than simply doing the work yourself, but it will be worth it. Making changes to create workflow ease will enable and empower you to take a step back, which will then free up your time and energy to focus on the most important parts of running your business instead of the mundane tasks that probably take up too much of your day right now.

In my service-based pet business, and for clients in similar industries, here is what basic automation looks like:

- **Utilize online scheduling and billing.**
  If you don't already have one, you'll want to sign up for an administration software system to automate your scheduling, reminders and billing. (Email me at Thrive@SFPBacademy.com if you would like the name of a software system I highly recommend.) There is no reason to be handling these time-consuming tasks yourself. If you have avoided signing up for administration software to save money, keep in mind that the cost of the software often pays for itself tenfold in the time and energy you will save!

  Even if you have an office manager or office assistant to help with administrative duties, having a software system that automates scheduling and billing will still be to your benefit because it will enable your office staff to more easily handle other responsibilities you are currently doing yourself. (If you don't currently have office staff, you will find more information about hiring office managers and assistants in Chapter Eight.)

- **Set up a business-only phone number and email address for business communication.**
  Many small businesses start as one-person operations, with the business owner handling all client communication on the go with a personal cell phone and email address. As the business grows, this becomes less and less sustainable. If your clients have your personal cell phone number or personal email address, begin weaning them off by directing callers to an office or business phone number and email address in your personal voice mail message or automatic reply on your personal email.

  As inconvenient as it may be to maintain two email addresses or phone numbers, you will never have the space you need from your business to regain your energy and creativity if you are constantly answering client calls or emails. It is also much harder to "turn off" your business side if you are constantly faced with work emails. I will cover the importance of setting office hours in the next chapter but having a separate business email is a vital first step in that process. It will also be easier to hand off email and phone duties to an administrative assistant or office manager if your clients are already accustomed to contacting the business instead of calling or emailing you directly. Also, if your main business email has your personal name in it (example: Kelly@abcpetcare.com), change that to a more generic beginning, such as admin, support, help, etc. This way, when you do hire a manager or office assistant, your clients won't be expecting you to respond at all hours of the day and your managers can use that email too.

- **Set out-of-office responses to business emails.**
  Before I had staff members, my work with pets took me out of the office most of the workday, so my automatic email reply encouraged clients to visit the website for scheduling/billing or call the office manager with other concerns. That allowed

clients to have their needs met quickly and helped me set specific times of the day to read emails, which then freed up a lot of my time and energy for the projects that were most important to the long-term health of the business without constant interruption. This was especially important early on in my business when I was the sole pet care provider for my company. I was free to work with the pets during the day without trying to also respond to client questions in the middle of a visit or walk.

Taking a step back from the minutiae of business operations will give you more time for other professional or personal priorities. It will be better for your business as well. As I mentioned earlier, just like relationships need a mix of personal space and quality time to grow, so too, does your business.

Setting up my pet business to operate without me started by automating as much of the administrative tasks and paperwork as possible. When I forced myself to take some much-needed time off, I did make less money at first, but I found I had much more energy to deal with my clients when I returned. Originally, I had been so stressed and overwhelmed that I'm sure I was turning people away without realizing it due to the exhaustion I was communicating with my overall demeanor. In fact, I discovered that once I set up my business to function in my absence, the more vacations I took, and surprisingly and happily, the more money I made!

Stop Using "Busy" to Describe Your Schedule and Your Life

The words you speak have power. You may be neglecting to tap into that power by constantly talking about how busy you are. When you run into a friend or catch up with family and they ask how life is going, how often do you reply with, "Good, but busy"? How often have you apologized to a loved one with, "I'm sorry I've been so out of touch; I've just been so busy lately"? It can become a habit to immediately turn to the word "busy" to describe your day and your life.

Here are a few examples of ways to change the paradigm of your language to focus on something other than how busy you are:

- The next time someone asks how your business is going, talk about what you are working on or what's going well in your business, instead of how busy you are.

- Instead of automatically thinking or saying, "I'm too busy to do that," tell yourself this instead: "I am choosing to spend my time in another way." While you may have to put a few goals, dreams or desires on hold at some point in your professional journey, realizing you are willingly making that choice to put them on the shelf for a bit goes a long way to preventing inner resentment and burnout.

- If you need to excuse yourself from a social event because you have a full schedule, simply decline without an explanation — don't use the crutch of busyness as an excuse.

- When you are busy all day long — and those days will happen — talk about the end result. "I have a lot going on this week, but I am really excited about how the project is coming together" shifts the focus from your busyness to what you are working to achieve in your life or business.

It may seem like an insignificant change to avoid talking about how busy you are, but your perspective will expand (and so may your time) as you focus on something other than busyness. In addition to the benefits to you, the people around you may be more forgiving and perhaps even feel closer to you when they have a better view into your current situation than the rote, "I'm so busy."

> **Burnout Recovery Tip**
> The more you intentionally avoid using how busy you are as a badge of honor, the easier it will be to step away from a constant sense of urgency.

If you feel guilty saying "no" but have the courage to do so in spite of feeling guilt, you are on the right track. Turning down an offer or opportunity is not the same thing as saying, "I have no more time in my day." Instead, you are saying (to yourself and perhaps others), "I am not choosing to spend my time and energy on that right now." That is a very powerful shift.

Contrary to popular belief, you can be a business owner and not be busy. Don't buy into the belief that you have to be busy to have or make money or sacrifice profits in order to have time for yourself. It IS possible to have both time *and* money.

Don't Use Busyness as a Mask for Other Problems

In my work as a business coach, I see clients so busy they are afraid to take a deep breath. In fact, when I've encouraged stressed clients to slow down to take a deep inhale and exhale during a session, they often tell me they are afraid to take a conscious breath. They have said they would rather push through their exhaustion and stay busy and stressed than stop and feel, which they suspect will happen when they finally take a deep breath. They are often afraid of the emotions, feelings and sensations that may arise if they are still for too long or connect to their body by breathing deeply. Rather than face that unknown, they choose (consciously or unconsciously) to stay busy and stressed and then wonder why they are so exhausted and overwhelmed.

In each of these cases, my clients are using busyness to cover up other issues they either can't or won't deal with. Being busy can mask other problems because of the adrenaline rush you may feel as you hurry from task to task. This rush of adrenaline that arises from busyness can be addicting and/or can numb feelings. For many of my coaching clients—and for me before I dealt with my own burn-out—being busy can be an "acceptable" way to avoid the more painful and inevitable parts of life. These overworked and overwhelmed pet business owners never allow themselves to slow down and take stock of their business, relationships or goals. Painful feelings are easy to push down and ignore when there is a never-ending list of things to do, which add bursts of adrenaline and urgency throughout the day, which in turn, often keep the painful feelings at bay. This can then become a vicious cycle: Painful feelings arise, so you may push the feelings down with busyness instead of taking a much-needed break from work. Eventually, you finish the work or feel the need for a rest and take a step back. At that point, like a beach ball that's been held underwater for some time, the painful, suppressed feelings will likely emerge with a lot of force, leading you to instinctually jump back into work as a way to avoid feeling the feelings. And so, the painful cycle continues unless you face it with courage and a willingness to be with your discomfort.

Pushing down feelings may work in the short term, but this avoidance is not sustainable. Your feelings and issues will force their way back up at some point... sometimes in the form of an illness, injury or pure and utter exhaustion, which will then force you to slow down. I have a client who noticed she would get sick right after completing time-consuming business projects. After some self-reflection, she realized that she was pushing herself through the physical warning signs and mistreating her body, but the adrenaline was carrying her through the stressful event. Then, like clockwork, she would find herself sick in bed when the stress let up. Instead of spending those days catching up with loved ones or enjoying some much-needed time away from work, she was ill and miserable. Her body was forcing her to slow down after too many weeks of pushing it too far.

A friend of mine had a similar experience. He worked diligently all through his chiropractor training, telling himself that he would finally relax after he graduated from school. Even when he would say, "I need a break" to himself or to other people, he would put off taking some time for himself and instead decide he had to finish school first before he could take that much-needed break. Then, a week after graduating from chiropractic school, he broke his arm and was unable to work for a few months! He got a break, but not the one he wanted. As I mentioned earlier, your words are powerful. If you don't give yourself needed time and space to rest, you may find your body gives it to you instead.

Ride the Ebbs and Flows

You may be reading this chapter and thinking, "That sounds great, Kristin, but my situation is different. There are times when I truly do need to work 12- or 14-hour days to make my business work." I get it. I've been there, and you might be right! Sometimes you *will* need to work long days no matter how many automated or other time-saving systems and strategies you've set up for your business. Starting, growing and running a pet business requires a lot of time and energy... especially at first. In the beginning, forging a path for yourself as an entrepreneur can often require at least twice the effort as a traditional

9-5 job. The key is to not let that pace become your new normal. After you've been in business for a while, it's important to wean yourself off the busy and time-consuming tasks—especially the ones you don't enjoy doing or aren't good at—and delegate as much as possible (or as much as you would like to delegate) so you can then step away from the parts of the business that aren't in your skill set or wheelhouse. Besides saving time in obvious ways, delegating can also save time in ways you might not expect. When we do tasks we don't enjoy or aren't good at, it can often take two or three times longer than it would take someone who was skilled at doing that task.

No matter how long you've been in business, there will sometimes be periods that will require you to be busy. That's just a fact in the life of a business owner. There may be seasons each year or a long stretch of time where you may need to focus most of your time and energy on your business. Emergencies and opportunities may crop up that require more of your energy. Even after you create space to step away from your business from time to time, not every single day will be perfectly balanced... but with a commitment to eliminating busyness for its own sake, your life can become more balanced over longer periods of time. Even if no one day is evenly divided among priorities, the months or years can be.

Kristin's Story

When I was working long days in my pet care business, my mantra to friends and family was often, "I'm so busy." It took a lot of time and conscious effort on my part to begin to shift my language and stop using the "busy" word because the phrase "I'm so busy" had become such a long-standing verbal habit for me. Even now, I will occasionally reactively respond to the question "How are you?" with the phrase, "My schedule is so full," but I'm even weaning myself off that phrase! It feels so much better to let friends, family and even strangers get to know me better and let them into my world by sharing something specific that's happening in my life or what work projects are captivating my passion, attention and time rather than the nebulous response "I'm so busy" or "My schedule is so full." They often appreciate the specificity too, and it also opens the door for them to then share with me the specifics of what's happening in their personal life or work.

Burnout Recovery Success Stories

"I've definitely embraced slower days and less travel. I raised my prices across the board and kept my social media game up. I go kayaking almost daily and I remember what color my husband's eyes are!"
Cindy Gingrey – Happy Dogs Pet Services
Gainesville, Georgia

"Email templates save me a lot of time and allow me to respond to clients quickly and professionally while also giving them extra information. I create a good-looking email and then save it as a template in my work email."
Stephanie Surjan – Chicago Urban Pets
Chicago, Illinois

"After writing up manual invoices for every single client, I'm now using software, which has made things a lot easier. I can now send invoices to the client before or after a service and not have to spend extra time adding in names/addresses/bank details etc. I can also see if they have any outstanding payments due or any credit!"
Natalie Durack – Happy Hounds Dog Walking and Pet Sitting
Gold Coast, Australia

"Automation has significantly allowed me to scale my business. I use a scheduling software, online forms, text and email as well as remote access so I can run my business from anywhere."
Karen Furtado – Shear Magic Pet Salon
Hilo, Hawaii

"Thank goodness for automation! I was literally doing everything manually up until two years ago. I got pet sitting software and it has everything I need: online scheduling, invoicing, schedules for the sitters and running reports. Everything all in one place. Genius! I also switched our clients over to online payments instead of leaving payments there for the sitters to pick up on their first visits. That was a fiasco as the sitters would pick the payment up and then have to drop it off to me – all time that could have been

spent doing other things. Our clients transitioned really well and the hours it used to take me to schedule, invoice and run reports was literally cut by 75%. I can now shift my focus to what is really important like networking the business."

Julie Gonzalez – Faithful Friends Pet Sitting, LLC
Cary, North Carolina

"Our software has really helped us automate. We can take bookings through the website. Our clients can also use the website to upload vaccine records, sign our service contract and more. This helps streamline our meet and greets and allows us to have less contact with our clients in their homes. We can now focus on their routine and pets by getting questions about our pricing, policies, contract and services out of the way before we meet."

Barbara Link – New River Valley Pet Sitting & Farm Services, LLC
Christiansburg, Virginia

"I have been working hard to make my business as automated as possible. It's still a work in progress, but my basic goal is to set the business up to be able to operate while I am asleep. Or better yet, when I'm on vacation! So far, clients can create their pet profile, review and agree to our policies and schedule a meet and greet all without me having to lift a finger."

Michelle Sabia – Paws & Claws Pet Sitting Services
Cave Creek, Arizona and Litchfield, Connecticut

"We decided not to run our business the way we did before the pandemic, which meant an entirely new set of policies and procedures. I hope my husband and I are strong enough in ourselves to abide by what we learned during the shelter-in-place.

Mainly what we realized is, for us, that there is 'no place like home,' being with each other and our family. We don't want to go back to the frenetic rat race of running ourselves ragged and being two ships passing in the night. We love the slow-paced home life we have created.

We may not be rich, but we sure are happier."

Cynthia Rinehart – PetzRFamily2
Napa, California

Action Steps – Take the "Busy" Out of Your Business

Action Step

The "Give Your Business Space to Breathe" section includes three specific suggestions for structuring your business to find more time in your day. Take a look at each item and consider how to update your current business accordingly.

In your burnout recovery journal, make your own list of three changes you can make this week to give your business space to breathe. If you do not have an online administration scheduling system set up to help you automate your client data and billing, email me at Thrive@SFPBacademy.com for my recommendation.

Action Step

How many times do you say, "I'm busy" in a day? Keep a tally on your phone or in your burnout recovery journal for the next 72 hours. Is the total more or less than you expected?

Then, for the rest of the week, focus on replacing "busy" with other words to more accurately describe your situation—without the crutch and subtle brag of being busy. Instead, describe what you are busy *with* or talk about the goal you are working toward. After a week, write in your burnout recovery journal how your perspective has changed as you've begun to eliminate "busy" from your vocabulary.

Action Step

Throughout the journey this book will take you on, I will encourage you to dig deep in your personal reflection. This will be your first opportunity to stop using busyness to mask other problems. Set your dedicated timer for 30 minutes and take time to reflect on your personal and professional life. What is going well? What are your primary sources of stress or disappointment in your business and in your personal life? Be breathtakingly honest with yourself. If you could make three changes in your life or business in the next year that would positively impact your quality of life, what would they be? What's one small action you can take today toward one of those changes?

FIVE

Protect Your Inner Peace

Set Boundaries with Clients and Prevent Compassion Fatigue Within Yourself

*"If someone throws a fit because you set boundaries,
it's just more evidence the boundary is needed."*

–Anonymous

In the first pages of this book, I promised a combination of strategies for shifting your mindset and practical business tips. This chapter is a combination of both. When I am coaching business owners, I often see a lack of boundaries drive them to exhaustion and burnout. The purpose of this chapter is to give you specific advice and the understanding you need in order to see why setting boundaries works to protect your inner peace without hurting your business.

Don't Let Fear of Losing Clients Control Your Choices

Decisions based on fear will keep you from reaching your full potential, regardless of whether the fear-based decisions are professional or personal. Instead of making choices based on what you are afraid of losing, allow yourself to make decisions based on what you will gain; decisions that will lead you where you most want to go in your business and your life. This does not mean ignoring your fears or pretending you do not have them; instead, recognize and acknowledge your fears and commit to stepping through fear to reach your desired result.

One of the most common fear-based mistakes I see my pet business coaching clients make is letting fear of losing clients or money prevent them from setting boundaries for their personal and professional lives. They will often choose money even if it comes with stress and strain over peace. Without clear boundaries, these same pet business owners fail to let go of difficult clients and run themselves ragged trying to meet those clients' impossible demands. They then may feel resentful toward their clients or their businesses for the fact that they are so exhausted, but rarely recognize that the frenetic pace is their own doing unless it is pointed out to them by someone else.

> **DECISIONS BASED ON FEAR WILL KEEP YOU FROM REACHING YOUR FULL POTENTIAL BOTH PERSONALLY AND PROFESSIONALLY.**

As you read through the rest of the chapter, you may find yourself thinking, "I could never set boundaries with my clients. If I do, I may lose a lot of my clients!" It's true, you may lose some, but they will likely be difficult clients who are used to demanding their own way. Once I realized how expensive difficult clients were to my health—my emotional and mental health as well as the health of my business—I saw that *not* setting reasonable boundaries with clients would cost me everything if I had to close my business due to burnout. Don't let fear stop you from setting reasonable expectations for your business and clients to protect your inner peace.

Learn to Say "No"

Do you have a hard time saying "no" even when you know you should? Many people do, especially in service-based industries like pet care. Most of us gravitate toward caring for pets (and their people) because we like to help and many of us are natural and skilled caretakers. That same generosity can make it very difficult for us to say "no" when we need to.

In her book, *The Fringe Hours,* Jessica N. Turner lists nine creative ways to say "no." Some of her examples are intended more for personal relationships and not applicable for the owner of a business, but her list got me thinking about my own ways to say "no."

Here are six ways I have found to say "no" to my clients when I need to reinforce a healthy boundary, along with examples of how I might say each:

1. **Just say "no."**
   "No, I'm not able to do that."

2. **Remind difficult clients about company policy.**
   "If you remember from the service contract, company policy prevents me (or my staff) from doing that."

3. **Give a recommendation.**
   "I can't help you, but I can give you the contact information of someone else who might be able to help."

4. **State your commitment to yourself and/or your loved ones and stand behind it.**
   "I've made a commitment to my partner/self/family not to take on any more projects/work/services right now."

5. **Offer another time.**
   "That sounds like something I would love to do! I am not available now, but I will have time to dedicate to it later this year. If you still would like my help, check back in about three months."

6. **Be grateful.**
   "I am honored you would think of me. I cannot accept at this time, but please know how much I appreciate the offer."

Not every strategy will work in every situation, but each of these ways to say "no" has worked for me at one time or another. In fact, you may even find it helpful to combine these options. For example, you can combine gratitude with an offer for another time: "I am so honored you would think of me, but I will not be available until later this year."

One note on giving a difficult client the recommendation of another pet professional: if you are turning down a difficult client, do not recommend them to another company without asking the company owner first if they would like to take on the difficult client; professional courtesy goes a long way. Be honest with them about your experience with the challenging client and let them choose if they want to take on the client *before* you pass on their name. If you are wondering why any pet professional would want to take on a difficult client, remember this: What makes the client difficult for you might not apply to another pet service provider. Be up front about the reason you are turning the client down and give another pet business owner the opportunity to make an informed decision before giving their name to the client you've decided not to help.

Five Steps You Can Take Now in Your Business to Protect Your Inner Peace

Your most important job is protecting your inner peace so you will have the energy and enthusiasm you need for your business and your personal life. Without preserving your internal balance, no amount of "life hacks" or business changes will fix the problems that are contributing to your burnout.

Here are five specific steps you can take now to protect your inner peace:

1. **Stop using your personal phone number or personal email for work.**

   As mentioned in the previous chapter, many business owners use their personal cell phones for business when they start out, often to save money or because they just don't have enough calls to justify the expense of another business-only phone line. However, it doesn't take very long to realize this won't work long term. Mixing personal and professional calls is a recipe for burnout because you can never get away from the business and your client needs. Also, as I mentioned in Chapter Three, it is equally important to have a separate email for your business, especially if most of your client communication happens through email.

   If you have been operating your business with your personal phone and email for some time, it may take a concerted effort to ensure clients stop calling your personal number or emailing you at your personal email address. Start by informing each client that you are moving over to a new business number and email. Then, set up a voicemail message that includes the new number and an auto-reply email that directs them to the new email address. At some point (I suggest no more than two weeks), stop responding to business calls and emails that come in on your personal number/email. If a few persistent clients still won't make the transition, you may need to consider getting a new number altogether.

Another benefit to a business-only phone number and email address is the ability to transfer phone and email responsibilities to an office manager or administrative assistant. If your clients are already accustomed to emailing and calling the business line, and if the business email is not your specific name, they won't be surprised to get a response from your office staff instead of from you personally.

2. **Set office hours... and keep them!**
   The most difficult part of setting and keeping office hours is often the first few weeks of your new routine. Once you set the precedent, clients will get used to it... and so will you. Set office hours by giving yourself a start and end time for each day's workday and commit to sticking with those hours. Except for true emergencies, there is very little that cannot wait until morning.

   I find it especially helpful to choose set times each day for checking and responding to email and voicemails. I often suggest my coaching clients state these specific time periods in their voicemail message, so callers know when to expect a response. By limiting your work hours and your message responses to set times or periods of time each day, you will free up your schedule, energy and enthusiasm when you are "off the clock" for your other life goals, self-care and important relationships instead of being in "business-owner mode" at all times of the day and night.

3. **Stop letting texts interrupt your work and personal time.**
   Texting can be a convenient way for business owners and their clients to communicate quickly, but it can also encourage blurred boundaries and lead to burnout because of the constant demand for your attention and the feeling that clients who text are demanding an immediate response. For these reasons, some business owners choose not to communicate via text at all. For others, texting is a vital part of the way they get

information to and from clients. If you do plan to keep texting clients as part of your business communication, read on for how to set boundaries without worrying about losing clients or missing important communication.

The main problem some of my coaching clients have with texting clients is that clients generally expect an immediate response, even if it is well after normal business hours. Just like you need business hours for phone calls and emails, set periods of time during which you will respond to text messages throughout the day. If you stop texting clients back immediately no matter the time of day or night, you will train your clients to stop expecting an immediate response beyond your regular business hours, except in cases of real emergencies.

> **Burnout Recovery Tip**
> Get to know your phone's do not disturb and silence settings. Being able to turn off notifications at certain times of day can help you maintain your office hours. Most phones will also let you set certain numbers as "always accept" if you are worried about missing a call in an actual emergency.

If you have clients texting you on your personal phone, set an autoreply to all texts that includes the new work number (and in your auto text reply be sure to specify whether that new work number can accept texts).

4. **Enforce policies and procedures.**
   How many policies do you have that you don't enforce? One of the most common unenforced policies among pet business owners is receiving a late client payment or accepting a last-minute booking without charging a penalty or fee. If you aren't currently accepting late payments without your clients incurring a late charge, don't start... and if you are, stop! Once clients know they can pay late or schedule last minute without penalty, some of them will set a new due date in their own mind or contact you last minute, rather than pay the full payment in a timely manner or give you adequate notice when booking an

appointment. Late or sporadic payments make it difficult to accurately predict future income and are a major headache for bookkeeping (both of which you will learn more about in the next chapter). If you've ever dealt with a client that habitually paid late or in partial payments, you know what I mean.

If you have fallen into the trap of allowing too much leniency when it comes to client payments, now is the time to change. Notify all current clients to remind them that all late or incomplete payments will incur an additional fee. Many of my coaching clients have found that charging a 10-15% late fee based on the invoice amount trains the late payers to pay on time in the future. However, be sure to check your local and state regulations and laws before you set your late fee amount. Some states have limits on how high a late fee can be, while others do not. If you aren't sure how to check that information, contact your local department of labor or a qualified business attorney.

Other policies often abused by clients if the business owner does not enforce them are last-minute cancellations, key drop-off or pick-up fees and extra charges for pet care during busy holiday periods. I also find that many clients come to expect extra services (such as nail trimming, administering medicine, key drop-off or pick-up charge or the pet sitter picking up pet food when the client's supply runs low) for free unless a charge is listed and enforced.

5. **Shorten your commute.**
   Many studies have shown that a long commute time is in direct opposition to satisfaction at work. The longer you spend sitting in traffic, the higher the toll on your emotional and physical health.

   When possible, limit your client radius to 20 minutes or less. I suggest you think of the commute in terms of minutes instead of miles, since the speed and congestion of the road makes a big difference in how long it takes to drive a certain distance, which can vary quite a bit depending on the time or day of the week.

If you have staff members, do your best to limit their driving radius also. I had many of my own new staff members insist they did not mind driving a long distance when I hired them only to find their enthusiasm waned once they made the commute for a few months. Everyone will be happier, and thus more productive at work if commute time is reduced to the shortest possible amount of time between clients.

Understanding and Preventing Compassion Fatigue

The reality of compassion fatigue really hit home for me and a number of pet professionals after the death of Dr. Sophia Yin, a well-known and much-beloved veterinarian and animal behaviorist. Her death by suicide was a wake-up call for many in the pet care community about the realities of compassion fatigue. I experienced some compassion fatigue myself when I had my pet care business, even though there wasn't that specific term for what I experienced at that time.

Since learning the name for this common ailment among pet business owners, I have come to recognize compassion fatigue and strive to prevent it in myself and in my coaching clients. The American Veterinary Medical Association has a very helpful article on the subject that includes the following quote from Dr. Frank M. Ochberg, a psychiatrist who specializes in trauma science: "[Compassion fatigue is basically] a low-level, chronic clouding of caring and concern for others in your life... Over time, your ability to feel and care for others becomes eroded through overuse of your skills of compassion."

Many people are inspired to start a pet business because of their inherent interest in — and concern for — people and their pets. But that same concern is often paired with a tendency to put their own needs last. In fact, psychotherapist J. Eric Gentry described it this way to the *Sacramento Bee*, "Animal care professionals are some of the most pain-saturated people I have ever worked with. The thing that makes them great at their work, their empathy and dedication and love for animals, makes them vulnerable."

If you are like many of the business owners I work with, you are probably nodding your head as you read those quotes. You know exactly what these experts are describing because you have felt it yourself and likely have also seen the impact compassion fatigue has had on other pet professionals. I have bad news and good news about this. First, the bad news: no one is going to swoop in and rescue you from the suffering you may be experiencing as a result of compassion fatigue. However, the good news is that you can save yourself! It is up to you to protect yourself enough to prevent your compassion from driving you to an unhealthy place of fatigue and even trauma. So many of the suggestions and exercises in this chapter—and in this entire book—are designed to help you on your journey as you develop a healthy relationship with your business.

Navigating Grief When a Client's Pet Dies

When a client's pet passes on, you will likely experience grief. Rather than bottling up the pain, consider finding ways to honor the pet and express your grief in order to heal. In the process of doing so, you may also help your client do the same.

In addition to the resources listed in *Recommended Resources* at the back of the book, here are a few ways that other pet care business owners have dealt with the passing of a pet and assisted their clients through the transition:

- Give your client a candle and a framed picture of their pet (or use adhesive to wrap the pet's picture around the candle).

- Donate money to a charity in honor of the pet.

- Send the client pictures you've taken during your time with their pet. They may not have yet seen or remembered these pictures and will enjoy a new perspective on their beloved pet.

- Create a blanket, pillow or mug with the pet's picture.

- Got other ideas? Please post your ideas in the Facebook group for readers of this book. Or, to find out more ways to deal with grief, do a search for "grief" in the private Facebook group: www.Facebook.com/groups/RecoverFromPetBusinessBurnout to see what other pet business owners are doing.

Grief comes in many forms, and even though it can be painful to acknowledge and face head-on, it needs to be dealt with. Ignoring the pain that comes from a pet or human client dying or having a favorite client move away just breeds problems down the road. Remember the beach ball analogy mentioned earlier? When we hold down our grief, it will inevitably come back up. The harder we try to bury it, the more it will come out sideways or straight up when we least expect it and knock us out! Dealing with grief intentionally will enable you to consciously work with it rather than letting it control you.

Become familiar with the stages of grief listed below so that you can recognize this grief when you see it in yourself or in your clients:

1. **Denial**

   Especially when the pet's death is the result of a long illness, this stage is generally brief, but painful. It can be difficult to believe that the pet is actually gone, both for the pet owner and for you and your staff who cared for the pet.

2. **Anger**

   This is a painful part of grieving because it is the stage when a pet owner or pet professional might blame the death on themselves or others. Anger can also be pointed inward and surface as guilt on the part of the pet owner or pet caregiver.

3. **Bargaining**

   Bargaining, often in the form of promising to make personal changes in exchange for a better outcome, is not always part of the grieving process after an expected pet death, but it is usually part of grief when dealing with a surprising terminal diagnosis or painful medical issue.

4. **Depression**

   It is normal for anyone who loved the pet who has passed on to feel intense sadness. In fact, if you've made it to this stage of grief, you know that you are processing the pain and moving toward the final stage...

5. **Acceptance**

   Everyone grieves differently and at a different pace, but eventually, if you have not buried the grief or run away from it, acceptance will come. It does not mean the pet is ever truly forgotten or the painful memories won't resurface, but it means that you have likely honored the loss by consciously grieving and have begun to heal.

Even if it's painful to face the grief head-on, that is the only way you will be able to heal and prevent compassion fatigue. As I mentioned in Chapter Two, even if grief makes you feel uncomfortable, don't go around the grief—go through it. If you don't, that grief will rear its ugly head in the future and come out when you least expect it, draining your energy and demanding your attention often at the worst possible time. Also, please be aware that grief is not linear. Your grief may start in a different order than is listed or go back and forth between stages. Regardless of how grief shows up for you, moving courageously and vulnerably through your grief, rather than around your grief, will likely help you get to acceptance more quickly.

Kristin's Story

One of the most difficult aspects of running a pet business for me has been the grief of losing so many animals I've grown close to while caring for them. One pet in particular that comes to mind was Jaeger, a Rottweiler who lived down the street from me. According to his human mom, Jaeger was not a barker, but when he would see me walking his next-door neighbor's dogs, he would bark. One day, I got a call from his human mom who said, "I think my dog wants you to walk him. He's not typically a barker, but whenever he sees you, he barks. I think he's trying to tell me to hire you!" I began walking Jaeger, and a love affair with both him and the breed of Rottweilers started with the very first walk. Jaeger was a gentle giant. He looked ferocious, as most Rotties do, but he was a complete and total lovebug.

I had walked him for a period of nearly two years when I got a call from his owner. She was crying hysterically as she told me, "Jaeger died!" I hung up the phone and ran down to her house where we both hugged each other and sobbed. Jaeger had a heart attack at the age of five years old. He died way too young and his death affected me deeply. It's been nearly two decades, and I still think about him whenever I see a Rottweiler; it's impossible for me not to.

Jaeger was just one of the many beloved pets I've lost during my years of being a pet care professional. I wish I could say that it gets easier, but that was never the case for me. Grieving is never easy. It's also not a linear process. I have found that when it comes to grieving a loved one, I don't just "get over it" after a set period of time, as much as I would like to have that experience. Also, each loss impacts me in a different way. Some losses are harder than others, depending upon my bond with the particular animal or human who has died. What's helped me get through the loss has been utilizing what I have shared in this chapter, as well as allowing myself the space and ability to let out the emotion when I need to. Holding it in is a recipe for inner turmoil, so as uncomfortable as it has been to feel the grief, feeling the sadness has been the catalyst to my healing.

Burnout Recovery Success Stories

"A year ago, I shrunk my daycare territory from covering all of Marin County to just servicing my town of San Rafael. I had to do this because the driving around and picking up of dogs all over the county was wearing on me and becoming unreasonable – in addition to the guilt I was feeling for driving dogs around for 1-2 hours during pick-ups before getting to my home for playtime. The same was true in the late afternoon and evening when I would be dropping dogs off to their homes. Inevitably there would be the occasional poo or pee accident from a dog or puppy who had not "emptied" prior to the ride. While I liked to think that doing the pickups and drop-offs myself made me the master of my time and provided a unique service to my clients who did not expect this of a daycare service, in actuality it robbed me of time I could have spent relaxed at home and it turns out my clients often preferred to drop off and pick up their own dogs.

For a few months, clients have been dropping off and picking up to/from my home and so a couple of weeks ago, I decided to permanently change my business policy and continue having clients transport their own dogs. Because I live in a neighborhood, I had always thought that it was less disruptive to my neighbors to have me do the transport. But what I have found over the past three months is that the comings and goings of my clients and their dogs are so brief that they actually cause no disruption at all and I, in turn, don't have to get up as early to get ready, am more relaxed just being in my home and not in traffic and feel a sense of gratification knowing that as soon as a dog or puppy is dropped off for daycare here they can begin playing."

Basia Tolscik – Marin Pet Care Pros
San Rafael, California

"I began enjoying slower times after the pandemic started. I had to set boundaries with my best client who refused to social distance and be safe. She cancelled half the walks because it was too much trouble for her to do a 'contactless' handoff. It's been very hard to set and stick to my boundaries when it means losing work. But in the end, my health and well-being are more important than caving to a client's whims."

Gini Chin – Jing! Go Walking
Portland, Oregon

"I made a number of changes in my business including enforcing cancellation policies. For a while, I had a 5-day cancellation policy for overnight pet sits. That meant that if a client cancelled their trip with less than a 5-day notice, they'd still get charged for the whole thing. This happened with a big-spending dog walking client and I ended up having to discuss over the phone why she'd still be charged. I told her that these services meant a big chunk of time and pay for my staff and that they need to feel safe that they'll be paid. It also gives them a chance to be rebooked by another client and not lose that pay. I'm happy to say, she still uses our services after that difficult conversation!

I also stopped using my personal phone number for business calls and I switched to Google Voice a few years ago, and it's been an important step toward delegating office duties to managers since they can access the number from any device. Since text messages appear in my email inbox, I don't feel worried I'll forget about it as I can mark it unread and find it later when it's time to respond.

I set office hours... and I keep them. Office hours are a great way to lighten the daily mental load. In the morning I can have breakfast and play with my toddler without worrying that a client is upset they didn't receive an immediate reply.

I've also shortened the radius in which my staff and I drive to client homes. This has been very important. With a smaller radius we can get to clients more quickly and therefore fit more walks in during the midday window. It's most difficult to implement when a good client moved out of the window of time, but I try to remind myself why I chose the neighborhoods we service and stick to it."

Stephanie Surjan – Chicago Urban Pets
Chicago, Illinois

"Setting boundaries involved shortening my service area and letting go of difficult clients. When it came to letting a client go, I reasoned that no amount of money was worth the stress of having a bad client and that has served me well and brought me more peace.

The best way I've found to deal with my compassion fatigue is to take time off. I take time off to be with my own pets, to talk to a therapist and to do nice things for myself like getting a massage or taking a vacation."
Este Cardos - Pawz and Palz Pet Care
Evanston, Illinois

"Setting boundaries has always been difficult for me in my personal and professional life. It's something I'm continuously working to improve! Recently, I had a client who was a repeat 'late payer.' She would continuously not pay invoices on time but add additional services and accrue more charges. Although I don't do my job for the money, I do need to be paid! I was becoming frustrated and overwhelmed providing these services essentially for free. I had to set a boundary, telling her that the invoice would have to be paid by a certain date before I could accept any more visits with her pets and that future invoices would have to be paid on time in order to continue providing services. Thankfully, she was very understanding. Although she ended up moving shortly after, she paid all future invoices on time!

Another boundary I have set is setting business hours for myself and having all clients schedule appointments through email or on my portal. This has given me more time to focus on ME and gives me more peace of mind. It also prevents me from burnout because I don't feel the need to be in the business 24/7!"
Ashley Farren - Ashley's Animal Academy, LLC
Downingtown, Pennsylvania

"A long-time client once asked me for a sitter's phone number. I told the client we don't give out the sitters' phone numbers and that all communication is now on the software messaging system. If there is a problem, she needed to call me. She was very offended and pushed back. I stood my ground. That was not easy to do! I am a people pleaser, and I felt like I was being a hard ass not just giving into her demand. On the other

hand, I didn't want the sitter to get the mixed message that it was okay to give out her personal phone number to some clients and not others. I felt fearful that the client would be mad at me, and I feared damaging the good relationship I had with her. But I also felt angry that she did not respect my boundary. In the end, she did come to accept the boundary because she had no choice."
Julie Fredrick – The Pet Sitter of Boise, LLC
Boise, Idaho

"I cannot even express how it saddens me when I hear of one of our clients' pets passing away, especially those that I have handled and cared for in the past. A perfect example was a client with a seven-year-old golden, Lulu. Oh, how I loved this girl so much. She was the sweetest pup I had ever had the opportunity to care for and walk. We spent a lot of time on trails hiking our hearts out. We really developed a bond. She would smile each time I would come to leash her up to go on our adventures. She got sick all of a sudden and was diagnosed with cancer. She died shortly after being diagnosed. It's been about seven years since she passed, and I still think of her to this day."
Julie Gonzalez - Faithful Friends Pet Sitting, LLC
Cary, North Carolina

"I had a couple different clients with constant last-minute scheduling that could have been scheduled way in advance, so I started charging an extra last-minute fee. While it's only $5, it adds up fast when they do it all the time. I also started saying 'No' occasionally, so they wouldn't take it for granted that I'd always be available. Lack of planning on their part does not constitute an emergency on mine. I now rarely have any last-minute scheduling that isn't a true emergency. I had to do something to end the stress of trying to squeeze in another client or having to change my plans last minute to accommodate theirs. I felt guilty about it at first... but enough was enough! It's okay to say no.

I also set the boundary of sticking to my office hours. I have clients who work odd hours and will text whenever it fits into their schedule. I used to respond, even if outside my contact hours, but now I realize they don't actually expect an immediate response. They know they are contacting me late/early/etc. and are fine when I do get around to a proper time to respond.

It was all in my head that everyone needed a response immediately. They don't! It's much more relaxing and I get more sleep!

I've also had several client pets die in the past few months. It's hard. Those pets are family, especially the ones I've worked with for years. I grieve. I cry (and cry). I up my exercise and usually wind up giving my own dog a lot of extra attention. Their lives are so much shorter than ours. When I do visits, I put everything into it because I want to have 'no regrets' in how I spent my time with that animal. I want to give them every bit of my attention while I'm there with them so that I know I did right by them and their family. They deserve that much at the very least, with everything they give to us. It helps, knowing that.

And it's weird... the animals I had an extra-close bond with and would see at least semi-regularly, I've known every time that it's going to be the last time I'll see them. I don't know if that's a blessing or a curse. It's been that way since I was a kid with animals. So, even though I already feel it's coming and I'm expecting it, it's still hard. I have a memory board in my office where I put up their picture and it's surrounded by little lights."
Brienne Carey - BC Pet Care, LLC
Wheaton, Illinois

"The most difficult client pet loss was with a 22-year-old cat. My client had Miss Kitty (MK) since she was a kitten and also had the monetary means to keep MK alive. I LOVED this cat, she was my baby too, but she was 22. We had birthday parties for her every year. Eventually, I had to tell my client it was time. She had the cardiovascular vet at her house, and he was talking about a complicated heart procedure. I had to tell her cats normally don't live until 22. My client is smart, but she needed to be told to stop. I would take care of MK often, and would have a bagel and coffee with her. She demanded my pat of butter, so I would always bring two pats of butter. I still have the last pat of butter that was meant for her. It is in my fridge with a note not to toss it. It is her butter. It has been three years.

Her mom and I talk daily because she has another cat, and that cat calls me nightly to meow at me. We still talk about Miss Kitty. It is good to talk about her and laugh about her. I have lost many clients over the years, but she is one that not only did I have to tell my client it was time to stop (which

she thanked me for doing later), but that I also took steps to keep reminders
of her. I have a million photos and stories."
Amy Sparrow – Furkid Sitting & Services, LLC
Baton Rouge, Louisiana

Action Steps – Protect
Your Inner Peace

Action Step

Cultivate the habit of saying "no." Look through the list of various ways to say "no" listed earlier in the chapter. For each of the six ways to say no, come up with your own examples of when and how you'd like to say no and list them in your burnout recovery journal. If you have any ideas of other methods of saying "no," add those to your journal as well. Practice the various ways of saying "no" out loud while driving or home alone. The more you can "work the 'no' muscle" by practicing it on your own, the easier it will be to say "no" for real with your clients.

Action Step

Set office hours for yourself if you haven't already. Establish a regular time in the morning to begin work each day and determine when you will stop checking work messages in the evening. Schedule in 1-3 times a day for checking and responding to emails and voicemails and let your clients know those times on your voicemail message and email footer. Find a friend or family member you can tell about your new office hours as a way to commit to keeping that schedule and so you have accountability if you are tempted to deal with work outside of those times.

Action Step

Go through your current client contract and look for policies you need to enforce more consistently or need to add to your client contract. If you are currently stuck taking late and incomplete payments, set a late fee and notify all your clients of the change. As I mentioned in the chapter, I recommend a 10-15% late fee, based on the invoice. Other policies to consider adding or enforcing are separate fees for administering medicine or trimming pet nails, a charge for key drop-off or pick-up or an hourly fee for any extra errands or additional chores pet care providers are often asked to undertake (such as purchasing more food or over-the-top plant watering requests). Don't forget to check your local and state regulations and laws for any cap on late payment fees.

Action Step

Find a quiet spot for self-reflection and set your timer for 15 minutes. Close your eyes and reflect on how much compassion and empathy you have for clients and loved ones. How might this compassion be negatively impacting you, your personal life and/or your business? Are you dealing with compassion fatigue right now? If so, what does that look and feel like for you? Are you experiencing unresolved grief due to the loss of a client (pet or human)? Use this time of self-reflection to write about your feelings and thoughts as it relates to compassion fatigue. Letting grief or compassion fatigue out and "speaking" to your journal pages may be cathartic for you and may alert you to a suppressed issue you need to deal with further. Be honest with yourself and be open to whatever may arise as a result of this exercise. After you're done, practice self-care by taking a bath, going on a nature walk, talking with a trusted friend or choosing another activity that helps you feel connected to yourself and/or another person.

SIX

Be a Conscientious Steward of Your Money

How Better Money Management Can Prevent Burnout

"When money realizes that it is in good hands, it wants to stay and multiply in those hands."

–Idowu Koyenikan

At first glance, a chapter on budgeting and tracking money may appear to be a big shift from the business burnout relief covered so far in this book. In reality, any changes you discover you need in your business will be easier to make (and evaluate) when you are in charge of your money instead of letting financial disorganization force decisions you'd rather not make. Money chaos is very destabilizing and exhausting for both the business owner and the business. Disorganization and chaos with money can include not paying bills on time (which then costs more money due to late fees), invoicing clients late (which impacts cash flow), and not separating business and personal banking accounts (which can create a lack of financial clarity), just to name a few. In my own business and in my work with business owners, I've witnessed that the way money is treated by the business owner is often reflective of organization—or disorganization—in other aspects of their business and personal life, not just the finances. When we clean up one major area in our business (like money management), we often naturally feel inspired to organize other aspects of our business and life as well. This overarching business organization can result in removing a lot of stress and strain that we may not even be aware is impacting our mental and emotional well-being.

Once you know your business income and how much your business needs to bring in to cover expenses, you will be able to more easily make informed decisions about hiring staff, taking time off work, setting and enforcing client boundaries and many of the other suggestions in this book. Knowing how much money you're bringing in each month and deciding where it goes can remove a lot of that fear and will let you make empowered choices instead of reacting to fear.

The Basics of Money Management

I am often surprised by the number of business owners who have no idea how much money their business is generating or expending. Without getting clarity on the money coming in and out of the company, their business will likely never be as profitable as it could be if the business owner was more financially organized. In this next section of the chapter, I'm including some information about basic money management so you can get a clear picture of how to be better organized financially. If you already have a budgeting system in place that is working well for your business, you may prefer to simply skim this part of the chapter and move on to sections later in the chapter. If you aren't sure if your system is really working for you—or you have a system that you already know isn't working—you'll want to read this section thoroughly!

Financial stewardship has three main parts: knowing how much you spend, knowing how much you make, and using that information to make informed and impactful decisions. First, you need to know how much money your business needs to operate, also called your "monthly nut."

The first step to determine your monthly nut is making a detailed list of the expenses your business incurs each month and year. Start with a broad list of expense categories. From there, you can add additional categories and specific expenses within each category. It may be easier to make separate lists for monthly and annual operating costs, so you don't forget to include expenses that occur less often (annual membership fees or business insurance, for example) and then combine them into one list.

Here are some basic categories to consider when making a list of annual business expenses, and you'll want to add additional categories that are unique to your business to the list:

Item	Annual Cost
Accounting	
Advertising	
Auto: insurance	
Auto: fuel	
Auto: maintenance	
Auto: payment	
Bank fees	
Business insurance	
Computer/ office equipment	
Contracted work	
Equipment	
Legal fees	
Licensing	
Membership fees	
Office supplies	
Parking fees/tolls	
Payroll	
Pet supplies	
Phone: monthly plan	
Tax payments	
Utilities	
Website	
Total Business Expenses:	

After you have completed your expense list, fill in the annual cost of each item in the column on the right. If you've been in business for longer than a year, use actual expense costs from your business for the last year to fill in this list. If your business is new or if you haven't kept accurate bookkeeping records (no shame, many new pet business owners don't), you may have to estimate some of these category amounts. Whichever way you approach gathering expense data, you want to end up with a specific amount that represents the cost to run your business for a year.

In addition to figuring out your annual expenses, it is equally important to know how much money is coming in — and from which income source. If you aren't already tracking individual income streams (dog walking, dog training, pet grooming, dog boarding, cat visits, etc.) for your business on a monthly and annual basis, start doing so. You may think you know which services are the most profitable, but until you are able to see the actual numbers, you may be making decisions based on inaccurate information.

I am writing from personal experience on this topic. Lack of clarity on what percentage of overall profit each service was bringing in almost cost me my business! At one point in my pet care business, I almost quit offering dog walking services because managing all the dog walkers and the scheduling felt like so much effort — until I sat down and actually calculated how much of my income was a result of dog walking. I discovered that dog walking brought in 42% of the annual business revenue. With that information, I decided to make dog walks more automated and an easier service for me and my staff to provide instead of doing away with dog walks altogether.

Burnout Recovery Tip
If you have staff who provide the same services as you do, be sure to create a separate line in your income spreadsheet to track income from the various services you've personally provided, as well as the income brought in by your employees. When it comes to taking charge of your money, the more information you gather, the better.

To begin this process of creating more financial clarity, utilize a simple spreadsheet in Excel or another program to record income for the last 12 months of business so that you begin to see what earnings you are bringing into the business as a result of services you provide clients and what earnings your staff are bringing in from their services. Your spreadsheet might look something like this, but with all 12 months of the year:

	January	February	March	Total:
Dog Walking	$1,000	$1,250	$1,305	$3,555
Staff	$750	$800	$805	$2,355
Owner	$250	$450	$500	$1,200
Overnight Sitting	$850	$920	$525	$2,295
Staff	$700	$800	$300	$1,800
Owner	$150	$120	$225	$495
Pet Visits	$1,295	$1,550	$995	$3840
Staff	$1,000	$1,250	$800	$3050
Owner	$295	$300	$195	$790
		Annual Gross Total:		$9,690

If you have administration or bookkeeping software, you may have access to an automatic report similar to this, without having to create your own spreadsheet from scratch. Whether you create a spreadsheet or use a generated report from your software system, you simply want to be able to see monthly and annual income totals organized by service and staff member. If you don't yet have a pet business administration software system, reach out to me and I'll share my top recommendation for an administration software system that many of my coaching clients use and one that I highly recommend. You can email me at Thrive@SFPBacademy.com.

Once you have your annual expenses and income organized in a way that makes sense to you, you will be able to make empowering and informed decisions about your money. Instead of experiencing free-floating anxiety and stress about whether there will be enough money, you will know exactly how much you have and how much more you need to bring in to meet your basic monthly expenses. As mentioned earlier, this information will help you find clarity as well as enable you to set definable monthly and annual financial goals for your business.

Make Ongoing Marketing a Priority

Some business owners think of marketing as part of the start or launch of their company — a task to be considered once and then set on autopilot. In reality, ongoing and diverse marketing is essential for the continued health and profitability of your business. Even if you're not currently trying to expand your business, engaging in regular, ongoing marketing will help you replace the inevitable client turnover, including clients who move or have another change of situation that leads them to no longer need your services.

When you aren't regularly marketing, you have to work twice as hard (and sometimes spend twice as much) in a short amount of time to try and get new clients. It can be stressful to have to suddenly expend time, money and energy to get more clients quickly. Whereas if you are doing "drip marketing" and regularly casting your marketing net wide with varied marketing streams, clients will begin to see your business everywhere. If you're reading this book, you're likely trying to lower your stress level, so stop marketing from the hip and instead be mindful and aware with ongoing marketing. Some pet professionals are resistant to marketing regularly because they are concerned they will have more business than they can handle. Yes, there may be times when you may have to turn new clients away, but even that can be a positive if you set up referral systems with fellow pet business owners in your area. Ask for a referral fee from local pet business owners for client referrals or ask them to repay the referral by sending you clients when your business is naturally slow. Then, when you need to add more clients, you likely won't need to scramble to find them. You can simply call upon your "pet business owner referral tribe" to send leads your way.

Here are three aspects of marketing to incorporate in your ongoing business plan no matter how long you have been in business:

1. **Focus on getting your right, ideal clients.**
   You may already know exactly what type of client you want to attract. If not, think about which of your clients have been the most (and least) enjoyable so far. What do your best or favorite clients have in common? Is it personality (friendly, generous, appreciative)? Location (close to your home)? Services requested that you enjoy providing? Another factor entirely? The ability to pinpoint what constitutes ideal clients for your business is essential in establishing a marketing plan.

Difficult clients cause a lot of stress and strain, which increases your burnout. Instead of struggling to appease difficult clients, work to attract your ideal client. And exactly who is your ideal client? If you can't easily answer that question, you won't be able to target your advertising effectively. If you don't know what kind of client you want, you likely won't be able to recognize it when it's right in front of you. Getting clear about and defining who your ideal client is — their habits, what they are looking for in a pet care company, where they are likely to come across advertising, as well as what was mentioned in the prior paragraph — will help you make the most of your marketing dollars.

2. **Track which marketing strategies are actually working.**
I've already written about how ongoing marketing helps prevent burnout, but only if you are focusing your advertising dollars in the most effective way. To do this, ask your clients how they heard about your business and then track what is working. By doing this, you might find you are surprised by the results!

One way to track marketing strategies is to add a question to your new client intake form asking how they found your business. Within a few weeks, you may begin to notice some common responses. You might also consider asking your long-time clients what attracted them to your business. I find that a quick email works well with a message like this: "Thank you for your business! I know you've been with us for a while and it may be hard to remember, but can you please let me know how you found my company and what made you choose us so I can continue to attract quality clients like you?" Record the responses in a spreadsheet for tracking marketing effectiveness if your administration software does not automatically generate a marketing report for you.

3. **Organize your marketing with a content calendar.**
A content calendar will help you keep track of advertising and social media updates, so you are not scrambling at the last minute to come up with a seasonal marketing campaign

or something to post online. With an organized calendar of topics, you can alleviate the constant stream of stress caused by trying to come up with what to post. You may only have a few minutes set aside to write a blog post on your website or update social media accounts. Don't waste that precious time staring at the screen, unsure what to write.

Instead, sit down two or three times a year to plan out your marketing and social media strategies for the next 4-6 months. Consider any future events or holidays you want to include in your marketing plan as well as any details, resources or links you (or clients) will need. Once you have content laid out a few months at a time, you can quickly glance at the calendar and know what to do with your valuable marketing time for the day.

Date	Topic/Title	Location	Links	Keywords	Notes
May 15	Vacationing with pets	Blog	Facebook, Instagram	vacation, pet sitter, travel with pets, pet-friendly hotels	link to "Top Pet-Friendly Hotels" post from last summer
May 20	Pets enjoying water	Instagram	Facebook, Instagram	pet pictures, fun with pets	
May 21	Announce pet photo contest	Newsletter	Facebook, Instagram, blog	pet sitting pictures, dog walking pictures, pet photo contest	
May 25	Keeping pets safe in the heat	Blog	Facebook, on the vet's website	summer heat, pet safety, pet care, pet sitting, dog walk	post already complete and sent over via email
May 31	Pet picture contest winners	Facebook	Instagram	pet pictures, contest, summer, fun	

This is just a basic outline of what your content calendar might look like, but it should give you some ideas in order to create your own. I recommend color-coding your posts by topic: green for how-to posts, orange for lighthearted and fun, blue for promotions, and red for expert advice. Color-coding allows me to quickly scan the calendar and see that I probably need some more varied posts in between the content already included on my calendar. I also know that it will be time for another how-to post near the middle of June.

Ongoing marketing helps the business grow in a way that is not overwhelming. If you need a more detailed list of low-cost and free marketing ideas, as well as a step-by-step process for creating a diverse marketing strategy and content calendar, see my book, *30 Days to Start and Grow Your Pet Sitting and Dog Walking Business.* Though it was written with pet sitters and dog walkers in mind, a lot of dog trainers, pet groomers and dog daycare owners have also used it as a guidebook on their journey to expansion and financial growth!

Why (and How) You Should Raise Your Rates

When was the last time you raised your prices? If it has been more than two years since your last rate increase, I recommend taking a look at whether you should do so now. The cost of doing business is constantly going up—from the price of gas to the cost of living—and failing to increase your rates will likely result in you working more hours each year to make the same profit. The goal of this chapter is to put you in control of your money, not the other way around. You won't want to raise your prices considerably for existing clients, but even raising your rates just a dollar or two (or whatever currency your country has) can have a positive impact on your financial bottom line, which could lower financial stress considerably.

> THE COST OF DOING BUSINESS IS CONSTANTLY GOING UP—FROM THE PRICE OF GAS TO THE COST OF LIVING—AND FAILING TO INCREASE YOUR RATES WILL LIKELY RESULT IN YOU WORKING MORE HOURS EACH YEAR TO MAKE THE SAME PROFIT.

If you are finding yourself running your business during an economic downturn, it may not be a good time to raise your rates. Use your own judgment and common sense. Pay attention to what is going on around you to know when your clients are ready for a rate increase. If the economy is challenged, it's okay to wait another year to let your clients recover financially before raising rates. In most situations, raising rates every 1-2 years is encouraged.

For example, if you are a dog walker, you'll find that increasing your dog walking rate by $2 per walk for just ten Monday-Friday dog walk clients will give you $4800 more each year without adding any more work or stress! Raising your rates by as little as $1-2 per service is manageable for most clients. This increase will give you more breathing room financially as you take back control of your life so that financial strain will not add to your stress and burnout.

One of the most common questions coaching clients ask me about raising rates is how to raise rates without losing clients. The fact of the matter is that you will probably not lose many (or any) clients by raising your rates slightly every 1-2 years. Here's why: a trusting relationship with a pet professional takes time to build and few, if any, of your clients will want to put in the work it takes to find someone new to care for, train, groom or board their pet all over again. In fact, I have had many coaching clients who had been fearful of raising their rates report back that they heard from clients who were surprised it had taken this long for their prices to go up!

I recommend you notify clients of your rate increase in a brief email. Do not apologize for raising rates and keep the email wording simple and to the point. Once your email is complete, include it with a regular newsletter (if you send one) or email it separately to your clients. Be sure to give them at least one month's notice before the increase goes into effect. You can find a sample rate increase letter along with other suggestions to help you increase rates on the "Free Stuff" page of my website: www.SFPBacademy.com/free.

Kristin's Story

Like most pet business owners, it took me many years after starting my business to raise my rates because I was afraid that clients would leave. It was challenging to figure out what to say about the rate increase and to know exactly how to do it in the way that would result in the least pushback or mass exodus of clients! What I discovered through trial and error when it came to raising my rates was only raising rates $1-2 for existing clients and using a short and sweet email to notify them was the best approach. I realized I could raise my rates more for brand-new clients if my existing clients were still below market rate after the small increase. Because it took me so many years to do my first rate increase, I needed to have a different rate structure for current clients than brand new clients. I realized the longer I went without raising my existing client rate, the bigger the gap would be between what new and existing clients were paying, so I got in the habit of raising my rates regularly every 1-2 years.

Burnout Recovery Success Stories

"This year I hired a financial coach to fully separate business from personal expenses and track them both. Since I've hired her, she and I have met online every week and this commitment, and the ability to talk frankly with someone about money and its fluctuations, has kept me grounded financially.

I reconcile my business and personal bank accounts every other day. It's easy and kind of fun. (I never would have said that before!)

At tax time, the online money tracking system I use will generate a report of all of the totals for each business and personal category. No more poring over receipts – they are already categorized and entered.

A couple of years ago I raised my rates across the board and only lost two clients. I have not looked back. I used to 'give away the shop' by discounting. Now I only give a discount for boarding that is three weeks or longer and then deduct just $5 from the usual daily rate."
Basia Tolscik – Marin Pet Care Pros
San Rafael, California

"I use QuickBooks to keep track of all business expenses/invoices. My personal finances are separate, and I use another app to keep track of personal expenses.

The hardest part about money management for me is keeping it all in one place and remembering to do it. I like that QuickBooks is pretty much

automatic, though I still have to manually send invoices and make sure it's all accurate and up to date. It's time consuming and no fun, but necessary."
Ashley Farren – Ashley's Animal Academy, LLC
Downingtown, Pennsylvania

"I use QuickBooks and a bookkeeper to manage and stay on top of my financials. The bookkeeper is the best money I spend each month. She's made such a huge difference for me!"
Shelly Ross – Tales of the Kitty
San Francisco, California

"Something powerful I learned from Kristin is the idea that letting go of difficult clients allows more room for my ideal client. By letting go of difficult clients, I also get my serenity back. It helps to take my emotions out of it and professionally type up the 'break up' letter if need be. If I really think about it though, I really haven't had to formally let a difficult client go. It sort of just happens on its own, usually after I have set a boundary. If they don't agree to that policy or boundary, I just don't hear from them again. Once I get clear on how I want to run my business and what my ideal client is, everything just falls into place just as it's supposed to."
Michelle Sabia – Paws & Claws Pet Sitting Services
Cave Creek, Arizona and Litchfield, Connecticut

Action Steps – Be a Conscientious Steward of Your Money

Action Step

If you don't currently track your business income and expenses on a regular basis, now is the time to start. Using the information under "The Basics of Money Management" section in this chapter, make two spreadsheets in Excel or another budgeting software: one for business expenses and one for business income. Be sure to calculate income by service and person (if you have staff other than yourself working in your business). After you have your income and expenses totaled, evaluate your average monthly income compared to average monthly expenses. Write down any positive or negative patterns you notice, including if any one service (or staff member) is responsible for more income than you might have realized.

Action Step

Set your timer for 10 minutes and write down any and all marketing and social media ideas as they come to mind. This is a great opportunity to record ideas that you have wanted to try but never had time to implement as well (this book will help you create more time!). This list will be an empowering resource as you create your content calendar and decide upon your marketing strategy. Use this list as a "master marketing list" and add to it in the coming weeks or months when more topics or content come to mind. If you run out of ideas before the timer rings, consider any upcoming holidays or seasons: are there seasonal or holiday promotions or campaigns you want to run during those times?

Action Step

As I mentioned in the chapter, ongoing marketing can help you build a safety net of new clients so that you are not scrambling to find clients when you have a spot to fill. A small amount of marketing every week is more effective (and much less likely to cause burnout) than one big stressful marketing push when you are desperate for clients.

Plan your marketing and social media strategies for the next three months by creating a content calendar that includes at least two items per week for each of the three months. These items might be social media posts, holiday or summer photo contests for your clients, blog posts or a new referral program. If any of your ideas are best suited for a guest post or require advanced preparation (extensive research, purchasing supplies, finding and hiring outside help, etc.), include those tasks on your calendar as well so you can plan accordingly. The items on the calendar in the next 2-3 weeks should be fairly specific so you know exactly what you need to do before implementing or hitting "post." Items that need more work or aren't ready to publish yet are better to include at a later date so you will have time to prepare.

Action Step

If you have been in business for more than a year and haven't raised your rates in a year or two, calculate an appropriate rate increase by comparing your rates to similar businesses in your area. An increase of $1-2 per service per year is a good rule of thumb, unless you offer pet boarding, overnight sitting in the client's home or dog training. In those cases, you may want to increase your service fee by $5. Then, compose an email to your clients notifying them of the new pricing structure. You can find a sample rate increase template on my website, plus gain many more tips about how and when to raise your rates. Scroll to the bottom of the web page to the link that says, "How to Write a Rate Increase Letter" on this page: www.SFPBacademy.com/free.

SEVEN

Master Your Time

Establish Routines and To-Do Lists That Empower Instead of Overwhelm

"The key is not spending time, but investing in it."

– Stephen R. Covey

Most of my coaching clients have strong feelings about to-do lists; in general, they either love to-do lists or dread them. Whether you are naturally a list maker or not, using your time efficiently is a vital part of running a business effectively. Learning how to get work done on time is a large part of that efficiency. Even if you think a chapter on to-do lists and time management isn't worth reading — either because you are already proficient at making to-do lists or because you don't like to use them at all — you might be surprised at what you learn in this chapter.

How Do You Use Your Time?

Before you can improve your time management and design a personalized time plan, you will want to evaluate how you are currently using your time. In the first *Action Step* of this chapter, I am going to encourage you to keep a time journal for at least one full week. Tracking how you spend your time in a typical week will give you a concrete starting point for all time management adjustments. You may think you know how much time you spend on paperwork or social media (either professional or personal), but until you have carefully tracked what you do, you will not know for sure. It has never been easier to keep an accurate record of how you spend your time thanks to any number of apps designed specifically for this purpose. You will find a few such apps in the *Recommended Resources* section at the end of this book.

YOU MAY THINK YOU KNOW HOW MUCH TIME YOU SPEND ON PAPERWORK OR SOCIAL MEDIA (EITHER PROFESSIONAL OR PERSONAL), BUT UNTIL YOU HAVE CAREFULLY TRACKED WHAT YOU DO, YOU WILL NOT KNOW FOR SURE.

By tracking your time, you will also figure out what your biggest interruptions and temptations are in the day. In an earlier chapter, I mentioned the benefit of setting specific office hours for returning phone calls and emails, but when is the best time of day to do so? Once you have tracked your schedule for one week, you will probably be able to find the best times of day for those tasks.

Creating an Ideal Time Plan

With the specifics gathered in your time journal, you are now prepared to create an ideal time plan. Start by making a current time map in Excel (or another program). This time map should outline how you currently spend your time.

Color-code activities with colors that reflect the most important parts of your time. For example, green might be for income-producing activities (marketing, returning client calls, doing the actual pet services, etc.) while pink may represent quality time with your loved ones. Once you have your current time map laid out, you can begin to modify it to reflect how you would like to spend your time instead. Some areas might not change at all, while others may represent a larger or smaller portion of your week's available time. I've included an actual example from one of my coaching clients (a dog trainer) at the end of this section.

In your ideal time plan, don't forget to include tasks you need to create time for, even if you aren't fitting them into your day just yet. Regular, healthy meals, meditation or exercise may be items you want to make more time for in your life. In the visual example I've included in this chapter, my client needed to eat more regularly in order to combat her burnout, so she added meals to her ideal time plan. She also carved out more regular time with her family and more blank space instead of scheduling every moment of her day.

Example Current Time Plan:

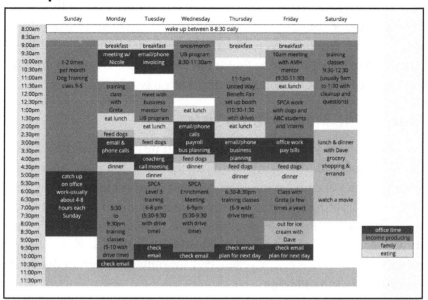

Example Ideal Time Plan:

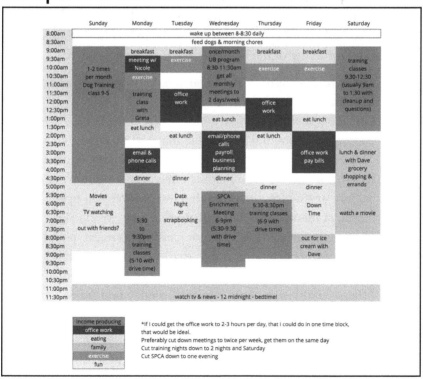

When you make your own ideal time plan as part of this chapter's *Action Steps*, remember to include lots of whitespace in your time plan. This activity is not about filling up your time but rather planning it in a way that works for you. Most of us (myself included) need large chunks of unstructured time that is not filled with activities in order to have space for the unplanned events of our day and life.

Making the Most of To-Do Lists

I have made it a matter of professional duty to make the most of my to-do lists and to help my clients do the same. Juggling the responsibilities of a pet care business, from client needs to managing staff to ongoing marketing and expansion, requires you to not drop the ball on any one aspect of the business. In fact, that constant pull in 20 different directions is one major cause of burnout for business owners. Making effective to-do lists is one way you can simplify the constant demands on your time and attention.

If you took one look at the title of this section and said, "To-do lists never work for me," you probably need to learn to write a better list. Keep reading to discover how.

Here are five steps I've used to improve my to-do lists that have also worked for many of the business-owner clients I coach:

1. **Learn to distinguish between what's important and what's urgent.**

   One metaphor that rang true for me from the book *Essentialism* by Greg McKeown was the idea that a to-do list is like a closet. Many people, unless they clean out their closets regularly, tend to accumulate too many clothes they don't really want or that no longer fit. Now imagine that every time you opened your closet, someone else had put more things inside. That's how to-do lists can be if we are not careful. So many people have calendars, expectations and to-do lists that are full of items that they don't want, no longer fit their life or were put there by others. Evaluating each item for urgency and importance is a large part of cleaning out your "to-do closet."

   The best way I have found to balance the urgent and important is to include both on my list each day. I suggest as you consider what needs to be done the next day, week or month, you rank each item in order of importance and again in order of urgency. When you finalize your to-do list, be sure to include both the most important and the most urgent items. By doing this every day, you will not fall behind on time-sensitive responsibilities while still giving yourself time to work on what is truly important for the long term.

2. **Make a daily, weekly and monthly to-do list.**
    Some tasks only need to be completed once a month or even once a year. I keep a running list of things that will need to be done over the next week and month and use that to decide what should make my to-do list for the next day. By keeping a written list of longer-term tasks, I free up the mental space to focus on something else instead of fighting that nagging feeling that there's something I've forgotten.

    Create a weekly and monthly list of responsibilities at the end of each week and month that you can use as you set each day's to-do items for that week or month. As you remember jobs that need to be done, you can quickly add them to the master list. I have found that after a few months of organizing my lists this way, it is easier for me to remember everything I need to add to my to-do list the first time. Like with most tasks, making a complete to-do list gets better with practice.

3. **Keep your lists simple.**
    I may have just recommended you keep three to-do lists (one for each day, week and month), but that doesn't mean each list should be long and overwhelming. If you are realistic about what you can actually complete in a day—and tracking your time for a week will help you know what is feasible for you— your to-do lists do not need to be daunting.

    In fact, if you try to do too much, you probably are not focusing on the most important work. Many people, especially business owners, are raised to believe that if we just work harder, we will be able to have it all. Instead of trying to do more or do it faster, I would encourage you to be more intentional about what you are working on in the first place. Consciously selecting your most important focus for each day will leave you feeling more productive than if you simply rushed through a mountain of tasks because the work you do will matter more.

4. **Give each item a deadline.**

   Have you ever opened a bill, taken a look at the due date and then set it aside, only to forget to pay it when the time comes? Or have you ever read a text message or email with the intention of replying later and then completely forgotten? Without deadlines, many to-do items will simply never get done. This is especially true of those important-but-not-urgent items I mentioned in Step 2. You may think of what needs to get done and even write it down, but without the accountability of a deadline, you may never get to it.

   I solve this problem by writing a deadline next to each item on my to-do list. I also include an estimate of how long each item will take. Then, if I find myself with a few free minutes between appointments, I can look at my list and see what I can do in that time. Assigning deadlines and time estimates has allowed me to avoid wasting time and forgetting important tasks.

5. **Start every morning with a plan.**

   Knowing your plan every day actually begins the night before. I write my to-do list each evening as I finish up work for the day so that I can begin each new day with my plan.

   Before I actually write the list, I sit quietly for a moment and ask myself how much time I realistically have in my next day for tasks and which tasks are most important to me. I regularly need to cut down on my list of tasks to make room for those items that have the most importance. Without that moment of stillness, I tend to add too many items to my list and often miss the opportunity to save less-essential tasks for another time.

Finally, I position my list in a place that I will see it first thing in the morning. I start each day with a cup of tea, so I place my to-do list next to my tea box the night before. Your best location will likely be different from mine but choose a place that will allow you to start your day with focus on what needs to get done.

The Importance of Knowing Your "Power Hours"

At the very beginning of this chapter, I wrote about how tracking your time will help you notice your biggest time wasters. Another benefit to logging how you spend your time will be figuring out your own best routine and which hours in the day are your personal "power hours."

What do I mean by power hours? I mean those two or three hours in the day when you are "on fire" and everything is running smoothly. Everyone's power hours are different, but almost everyone has them. You may already have some idea of when these hours are for you if you think about times when your ideas and energy are most flowing as opposed to when being creative or productive feels like a slog through drying cement.

You may have noticed a difference in power hours if you've spent a lot of time with someone else, such as a lifelong friend, a spouse or a partner. Many couples have different productivity cycles in the day and figuring out how to respect each other's natural rhythms is one part of making that relationship work, especially if you both work from home.

Here are a few questions you can answer to determine—or confirm—when your power hours are each day:

- When do you feel the most fired up to work?
- When do you feel the least enthusiastic about work?
- What part of the day is generally the most productive for you?
- If your work is interrupted, when is it the most disruptive?

Once you know your personal power hours, whether by evaluating your time log or by answering these questions (or both!), do everything you can to protect those hours. These should be your sacred work hours that are not interrupted except in the case of an emergency. You may need to rearrange your personal or family routine in order to give yourself that time, but it will be worth the effort because you will likely get so much more done in those special hours than any other part of the day.

Kristin's Story

A few years ago, I realized my power hours were in the morning, which is also the time of day I was most likely to exercise. Often, if I didn't exercise in the morning, it just didn't happen later on in the day. It was confusing for me to know what to do during these few sacred hours — should I work or work out? They were both equally important to me. Finally, I decided to exercise early in the morning before dedicating my power hours to work. Although my workout occasionally overlapped with the beginning of my power hours, I would be so motivated to get going on my work tasks with my workout done and a full day still ahead of me.

It's important to get creative when it comes to figuring out how to structure the times when we're naturally more productive. When we have multiple priorities vying for those few precious power hours, it's even more important to figure out how to make it all work.

Burnout Recovery Success Stories

"Working full time and trying to establish this business, I have very little time for organization, so I set myself small goals weekly so that I avoid being overwhelmed. I might set a goal to update my customer list and work on filing, for example. I create a weekly to-do list to help keep me on track and cross things off as I complete them. If they don't get completed, they get a new due date for the next week."
Barbara Link – New River Valley Pet Sitting & Farm Services, LLC
Christiansburg, VA

"My creative juices flow really early in the morning between 3-5 am. It's quiet and I can really concentrate on the task. Most of the Mainland is up and ready by then, so I often get phone calls during that time because people forget I'm in Hawaii. I have a lot of virtual meetings and live videos from the East Coast which is a 6-hour difference, so it helps that I'm an early bird."
Karen Furtado – Shear Magic Pet Salon
Hilo, Hawaii

"I write everything down as it comes to me. As a result, I now have at least three sheets of lists dotted around, probably more. I then go through these lists and try to make one list in order of importance, but then I find the amount I need to do totally overwhelming! I love ticking things off my list; there's something very satisfying about that, but it seems endless. On reflection, I think I need to make shorter lists!"
Kirsty Everard – Kirsty's Paws
Bournemouth, United Kingdom

"My power hours are early, and usually it's just a single power hour – the first hour of work each day. My least productive time is right after lunch when I am trying to reset my schedule, reorganize my desk and figure out where I am in my workday. I have ADD but cannot take meds, and one of my bad habits is having notes all over the place, including sticky notes, tablets, computer and binder. I know I write things down but remembering where I put the note is often the issue, so I tend to spend time reorganizing to update my desk from the morning's work in the afternoons."
Amy Sparrow – Furkid Sitting & Services, LLC
Baton Rouge, Louisiana

"For me, my power hours depend upon what the work is that I'm doing. I tend to be more productive making phone calls and talking on the phone before noon, and preferably, as early as possible, to get it out of the way. I use social media to get inspired throughout the day. I do office work and manage client updates throughout the day as well, but in a more focused way at three points during the day: in the morning, midday and evening. Some days I tend to be more productive getting office tasks done, like responding to client messages and processing service requests in the evening once I have settled down for the night. What makes it so easy to do this is I do it while relaxing and often while I'm watching TV. That way, it's almost as if it's not really work at all. As you can see, I am pretty all over the place with when it's best to get work done. My power hours definitely depend upon what task I'm doing.

I have come to realize that it's not specific points during the day that I am most or least productive but rather what days during the month. As a woman, my body functions at 28-day cycles rather than 24-hour cycles. I have been learning how my body goes through four seasons every month and

how that applies to how I get things done. I tend to be more outgoing and want to socialize and talk during the time I'm ovulating, for example. I'm also of course more emotional during this time, so my creativity definitely gets sparked and sometimes I have so many ideas I can't write them down fast enough! This is still a huge and exciting learning process for me as I continue to read about it and experience it for myself."
Michelle Sabia – Paws & Claws Pet Sitting Services
Cave Creek, Arizona and Litchfield, Connecticut

"I have a to-do list, though it's not usually broken down by day/week/ etc. It's just a long list that I keep adding to and crossing off. When it gets messy, I rework it. Anything that is more of a 'now' thing that needs to be done right away, I write in my planner for that day. My Passion Planner is my lifeline – if I put it in my planner, then it must be done. It's weird how that works. I see it there, so I do it.

As for my power hours, I am the most productive before 1:00 pm, so I always leave time in the morning for things I need to get done after morning visits and before middays begin. I try to leave myself a two-hour window at the very least. That's when I am the most awake and have the most energy. I am the least productive between 1-5 pm, when I start getting sleepy and need a nap if at all possible, or at least some downtime! I do sometimes get a second wind between 6-9 pm for anything I need to finish up. During my productive period, I go through my online classes, any paperwork and any cleaning that needs to be done that day."
Brienne Carey – BC Pet Care, LLC
Wheaton, Illinois

Action Steps – Master Your Time

Action Step

Keep a time journal using a time tracker app from the *Recommended Resources* section. For the next week or 10 days, take a few minutes at the end of each hour to log what you did during that hour. Keep track of your energy levels or any distractions that interrupted your focus during that time.

If you record any periods of an hour or more when you are able to work without distraction, make a special note of those, as they may be clues about your personal power hours. Also, as you'll see in the *Recommended Resources*, Focusmate Virtual Co-Working is a great resource for productivity, accountability and support. There's also a Focusmate group just for pet business owners! Visit this page to find out more: www.focusmate.com/signup/ProsperousPetBusiness.

Action Step

Using your time journal and the example given in this chapter, create a current time map and an ideal time plan. Be sure to include any tasks or activities you are not yet fitting into your day that you want (or need) to do to prevent future burnout, including daily exercise, regular self-care or dedicated time with family. In your burnout recovery journal, answer the following questions: (1) How does your ideal time plan differ from your current time plan? (2) What needs to happen in your business as it is being run now to make your ideal time plan a reality?

Action Step

Set aside 30 minutes to brainstorm all of the tasks you need to complete in the next month. With practice, you may find you need less time to make each monthly list, but this first time may take you the full 30 minutes. During that time, check any due dates during the upcoming month, as well as think about where you would like to be personally or professionally one month from now.

Once your list is complete, rank each item in order of importance and again in order of urgency. You will use this list as you make your weekly and daily to-do lists moving forward.

Action Step

Make a daily to-do list for the following day every night this week. Remember to include both important and urgent tasks and to assign each a deadline and a time commitment. Limit yourself to no more than five must-do tasks (or whatever the number is that you find is feasible without overwhelming yourself) each day. Place your completed to-do list in a location where you will see it first thing in the morning.

Action Step

When are your personal power hours? If you aren't sure, go back to the questions listed in this chapter under "The Importance of Knowing Your 'Power Hours'" and through your time tracking app to look for patterns of when you are most productive.

In your burnout recovery journal, identify your personal power hours and how you plan to protect those hours each day. If you need to wake up earlier, arrange for childcare, reschedule meetings or appointments or complete some other action to block off those hours, write down what you have to do and add those tasks to your to-do lists this week.

EIGHT

Hire and Manage Staff

Outsource and Delegate to Help You and Your Pet Business

"The important thing about outsourcing is that it becomes a very powerful tool to leverage talent, improve productivity and reduce work cycles."

– Azim Premji, Chairman of Wipro Limited

As you can imagine, the topic of hiring and managing staff is more complex than can be taught in one chapter. In fact, I wrote an entire book on the topic, *The Hiring Handbook for Pet Sitters and Dog Walkers,* if you need more specific hiring guidance. Even though I won't be able to cover every single aspect of hiring and managing staff in this chapter, I am including the basics because how you delegate responsibility has a lot to do with healing and preventing burnout. Depending on whether you've hired staff for your business yet—and if you have, how many and what kind of staff members are currently working for you—you may find some parts of this chapter more applicable than others. As with every other part of your burnout recovery, glean what you need now and save the rest for another time when you may want to revisit these topics again.

Hiring Helps Prevent Burnout

There are many reasons a pet business owner might decide to hire staff, many of which are directly related to preventing and curing burnout. Hiring the right people to help you with your business has many advantages. Letting quality staff share the workload will give you time and space to focus on long-term priorities and be the visionary, instead of always being stuck in the day-to-day work. You will also have more time in your personal life to do the important work that has nothing to do with your business.

I first decided to hire help for my own business when I realized I couldn't do it all myself. Not only that, but I also realized that *I didn't want to do it all.* When I started building my business to run without me there to oversee every minute of every day, I discovered something important. While I had started the business because I love animals, caring for them seven days a week was exhausting.

So many of the suggestions in this book depend on you having the time and mental energy to make positive changes in your life and business. If you are so busy with the constant demands of your business that you can't imagine taking an hour or two each day for rest or self-improvement, hiring may be the first step you need.

In my book on hiring that I mentioned earlier, I gave readers a list of nine signs they needed to hire help. Of those nine, four directly relate to burnout, so I am including them here.

Go through this list and ask yourself how many of the following ring true for you:

1. **You are losing your passion (and your patience) for your business.** When I started my pet care business, I was excited about doing the work I loved and being my own boss. A few years in, however, I found I had lost my enthusiasm. Even though I still loved my pet clients (and their humans) and enjoyed the freedom of being self-employed, I was no longer excited about my business. If you feel like you've lost the passion that drove you to start your business in the first place, you may be trying to do too much on your own.

> IF YOU FEEL LIKE YOU'VE LOST THE PASSION THAT DROVE YOU TO START YOUR BUSINESS IN THE FIRST PLACE, YOU MAY BE TRYING TO DO TOO MUCH ON YOUR OWN.

2. **You feel like you can't take a day off without your business suffering.** Vacations and sick days are impossible for pet business owners who do all the work themselves. Hiring the right employees will give you more time for yourself: the ability to stay home and take care of yourself when you are ill, freedom

to take a vacation without losing income, and time to simply take a day off to rest.

3. **You spend more time putting out fires than working on what's truly important.** It can be very easy to spend so much time juggling the demands of office work in addition to providing pet services (not to mention dealing with urgent issues that arise daily) that you don't give yourself enough time for other professional or personal ventures. Urgent work, such as returning client calls and emails in a timely manner, often crowds out the most important tasks that don't have pending deadlines. Hiring employees to share the workload will give you the time you need for less urgent (but more important) tasks.

4. **You feel annoyed, discouraged, or overwhelmed by all the work you have to do.** Do you feel a jolt of anxiety or frustration when the business phone rings or an email comes in? When you start your work each day, are you excited or annoyed? Evaluating how you feel throughout the workweek will give you a clear picture of whether or not your business needs more staff members to help with the work.

If reading through that list has helped you see that you do need to hire help for your business, or to hire more if you already have staff, the next priority will be figuring out how to hire the *right* people — staff members who will be self-starters and relieve some of your stress, instead of adding to it.

Help Your Staff Self-Manage

While hiring staff members can free up time for you, that's only true if the staff members are not constantly demanding your attention and help. Encouraging staff members to self-manage comes down to three different issues: (1) hiring the right people, (2) building trust between staff and clients and (3) giving staff the support they need.

1. **Hire the very best.**
   When I help coaching clients through the process of hiring, I always recommend they utilize a full application packet instead of a simple one-page job application or resumé. An application packet is often so successful precisely because it requires more

effort than merely submitting a resumé. It necessitates time, work and commitment. The applicants who are willing to fill it out and send it back to you show dedication right from the very beginning.

When you hire in your own pet business, you want committed applicants who are professional and pay close attention to detail. You will be able to see which applicants have these characteristics simply by reviewing their packets. Pay close attention to their responses and you will know a lot about them before you ever meet. You will get a higher caliber of applicants as a result of integrating an application packet into your hiring system. I guarantee it.

If you want more specific information about what I included in my application packet when I was hiring pet care staff and how to use it in your own business, you will find it on my website: www.SFPBacademy.com/packet or in my book, *The Hiring Handbook for Pet Sitters and Dog Walkers*. The application packet template found on my website can be customized for all different types of pet businesses.

2. **Show your clients they can trust your staff.**
   Some clients may be upset that you're not doing all (or in some cases, any) of the actual pet care service for them. There is a reason they chose you as their pet professional in the first place. It is up to you to show your clients that your new staff members are trustworthy and capable in the way that you introduce them and make the transition from doing the work yourself.

   When it comes time to introduce a new staff member to your current client, be confident going into the conversation. Be very clear with clients, without actually stating it, that this change is not negotiable. For example, if you're a dog walker, you can tell your client you will still be walking their dogs on Monday, Wednesday and Friday, but that you are no longer available on Tuesday and Thursday. Then, tell them that you would love to set up a time for them to meet the new hire you've made, and start telling the client what makes your staff member great.

Even though they might be resistant to someone new, it's pretty rare that a client will leave your company instead of working with your new staff member, especially if you have someone that you stand behind and can highly recommend... this is where hiring the very best staff members is key. You want to feel great about your new hires so that you can honestly tell your clients how wonderful they are. That enthusiasm will carry through your voice and put many of your clients at ease. They trust you and they will often extend that trust to someone you recommend so highly.

3. **Support your staff.**

Hiring and training new staff members is time-consuming and can be expensive. Ideally, you want as little turnover as possible, which is yet another reason that I encourage using a comprehensive application packet as part of the hiring process.

You can also encourage your staff members to stay for the long haul by giving them the support they need to be successful. Make sure your staff members know exactly what they need to do (and who/when/how to ask for help if they need it) before they start any solo jobs.

Establish a clear procedure for complaints, concerns and emergency contact. That way, if a problem arises, your staff will know the appropriate way to handle it with you. While you don't want staff members calling or texting constantly with small concerns (that would defeat the purpose of hiring help, after all), it is important to give them a proper channel for items they want to discuss. Let them tell you what they need and how you can make their work environment better. In many cases, it will not take much on your end to make the change, and your staff will be much happier for it.

Hiring Other Help

Hiring help is not limited to staff who assist with various pet services. One of the best things I did in my own business was to hire outstanding office assistants and office managers. During the years I owned my business and regularly traveled abroad, I had as many as five office helpers running the business while I was out of the country for months at a time each year. A skilled administrative assistant or office manager will be able to answer phone calls and emails, schedule new client interviews, update the staff schedule, order office supplies or schedule repairs and handle all the important situations that can crop up without warning. Just imagine how much time will open up in your schedule if someone else is handling all of those tasks.

Look for an office manager or assistant who has applicable work experience, is friendly with clients and staff, has a track record as a good communicator, can demonstrate organization and efficiency, has the ability to write with good grammar and spelling and is able to calmly handle emergencies with common sense. Many of my best office managers started as pet care staff in my business, so you may want to start your search with staff you already know and trust.

In addition to hiring office staff, you may want to consider hiring out tasks in your personal life. In many cases, the money you spend "giving away" tasks you dread will be justified by the creativity and energy you get back. Often, you will actually make *more* money once you are able to focus on more important decisions, even after you factor in the cost of this extra help.

Here are some other types of help you may consider hiring as part of your burnout recovery:

- An accountant and/or bookkeeper
- A housecleaner
- Childcare provider and/or tutor
- General maintenance help
- A cook to do menu planning or meal service
- Grocery delivery
- Laundry service
- Personal shopper

Many of the items on this list would have been considered extravagances in earlier generations but are increasingly more common and affordable now. There are mail-order meal services, clothing and design companies and more that allow you to try their items at home for relatively low fees. Grocery delivery, for example, has become commonplace in many areas and, for a small fee and the cost of a tip, can save you hours of driving and shopping.

If you aren't sure where to find this extra help, check the *Recommended Resources* section at the end of this book.

How Delegating Really Works

"Delegation" is a common buzzword in business and entrepreneurial circles as business owners try to figure out how to let go of being involved in every aspect of the business, no matter how big or small.

I often get questions from pet business owners who recognize they need to delegate but don't know what that really means. Others are finally ready to give more responsibility to their staff members but aren't sure how to go about doing so.

When it comes to actually delegating responsibilities, I have broken the process down into four actionable steps:

Four Steps of Delegation	
I DO, YOU WATCH	Observation
WE DO	Collaboration
YOU DO, I WATCH	Evaluation
YOU DO	Delegation

1. **Make room in your schedule.** One of the main reasons small business owners don't delegate, other than fear of losing control or losing clients, is that many tasks are simpler and faster to do themselves than to teach someone else how to do them. Because they are unwilling or unable to devote the time needed for delegation and training, they never let go of those tasks. To avoid falling into this cycle, make it a point to set aside time for delegation in your schedule by giving yourself a specific block of time each week to make delegation decisions and complete any of the tasks outlined in this chapter.

2. **Pick the right tasks for the right staff member.** By the time you've evaluated their application packets, interviewed each candidate, and trained each new hire, you will know your employees very well. Use your knowledge of each staff member and their skill sets when you decide how to delegate responsibilities. They will have more success and fewer complaints with tasks that match their skills and interests... and, as a result, you will be called in much less often to fix problems.

3. **Communicate, in detail, what you expect.** When delegating responsibility, be clear in your instructions so that you and the staff member have the same understanding of exactly what you're expecting them to do. One step I recommend pet business owners take in preparation for delegation is to make a list of everything you personally do when you are completing the service or task you plan to assign to someone else. Make a bulleted list of exactly what that service entails. A lot of the time, we are on autopilot when we're doing something we've done hundreds of times before, rather than thinking in terms of how to clearly communicate the steps to someone else.

   This holds true outside of business staff. If you are using a personal shopper to pick new clothes, for example, the more specific feedback you give your shopper, the better the selections will be. If you want a bookkeeper to help with your business finances, clearly discuss what you expect with your bookkeeper so there are no misunderstandings about what will (or won't) be done.

4. **Set a deadline and follow up.** While the goal of delegation is to move tasks off your schedule to allow you more time for yourself and for nurturing your business, it will still be up to you to keep tabs on what is getting done. Establish deadlines when applicable and schedule a time to follow up and see how the work is going. You will need to check in more regularly

150

with staff taking on new responsibilities—maybe as often as right after the first appointment or task—but you can follow up less frequently with more seasoned staff.

Checking in with team members taking on new tasks will give them an opportunity to ask questions, give you peace of mind that everything is going well, and allow you to celebrate successes or fix problems when needed.

Mastering the skill of delegation does not come easily for many business owners, but it can be done. Once you figure out how to delegate in the best way possible, you will probably be amazed at the extra time and mental space you have for the most important parts of your business and life.

Kristin's Story

When I was in the beginning stages of delegating, I made a list of all the tasks I was responsible for in my personal life and business. Next to each task were two columns. I marked in the columns a) whether or not I enjoyed the task and b) how much time it took to complete the task. If the task demanded a lot of my time and I didn't enjoy doing it, I automatically delegated that task to someone already working with me or hired someone new to do it.

One of the most time-consuming business tasks was returning phone calls and emails so I hired an office assistant to help me return phone calls and emails and to manage staff. My assistant started off just working two days a week, but as she and I grew more confident in her ability to run the business, she worked in the office four days a week and I worked three days.

Burnout Recovery Success Stories

"Hiring has definitely helped me recover from burnout. I love having staff! I only have one person right now, but I plan to hire a backup person soon. The person I have has been tremendous. She is flexible, learns quickly, has a lot of experience with a variety of pets and just knowing I can rely on her has made my life so much easier.

Having her on staff allows me to have a much lighter schedule so I can spend more time at home and with my own pets. I get a lot more done with my business as well. I've taken a couple of classes, for example. I work a full-time job on top of my business, and I used to leave at 6 in the morning, sometimes 5:30, to go do clients' pets then go to work. My employee now takes all of the morning shifts so I can get up at a reasonable time and take proper care of my own pets and myself. I don't feel as stressed since I know if I want to spend time with family or go somewhere, I can have her step in at any time as well."

Barbara Link – New River Valley Pet Sitting & Farm Services, LLC
Christiansburg, Virginia

"Handing off all evening visits to an employee was a huge freeing step for me. Next was handing off all morning time-specific visits, allowing me to concentrate on running the business. It's also a wonderful feeling to be able to pay people to do a job they really love. That's been my favorite part of hiring people.

I've been really fortunate with hiring. This past year, I was actually using a recruiter and having them screen and do initial interviews helps tremendously. I'm finding that farming out things I don't enjoy/I'm not good at is worth every penny I spend having it taken care of.

Outside of people to do actual visits, my bookkeeper is the absolutely best money I spend. I could never keep up with it and was always trying to pull everything together at the last minute. It was awful. My bookkeeper is WONDERFUL and takes care of everything. I go in and review (in detail because I'm a control freak), but she has made my business life a thousand times easier."

Shelly Ross – Tales of the Kitty
San Francisco, California

"A couple of years ago I was really on the verge of burnout. I was walking dogs from 10-4 Monday through Friday, pet sitting overnight every night of the week and doing dog training lessons in the evenings, plus trying to keep up with administrative tasks. This is probably normal, but I was terribly afraid of hiring new employees. I had built up such a loyal client base who relied on ME and my animal knowledge/experience that bringing new people in to handle their pets was very scary (especially the fearful/nervous ones). How do I introduce employees to every client and every pet? I fought that fear with education and actually by reading Kristin's Hiring Handbook

for Pet Sitters and Dog Walkers *book! The more I learned and the more I realized how much good would come out of it, the more I WANTED to hire. I decided to hire two dog walkers to take over my Monday- Friday 10-4 shift and it immediately helped my burnout. I felt so much less stressed because I had more time to focus on administrative tasks during the day and wasn't in a rush all the time!*

However, I have also had the experience of staff adding to my burnout. I am still a very small business with few staff. I hired a pet sitter for my AM/ PM drop-in sits. It was the middle of summer and although a pretty light summer, we still had quite a few upcoming visits. My new hire went through the training process and I put her on the schedule for upcoming visits. Unfortunately, she decided the job was not the right fit and quit at the end of her training process, leaving me to have to cover the visits I scheduled her for. This was obviously immensely stressful, but a lesson learned on my part.

That hire definitely cost me time, energy and money. I made the mistake of hiring partially out of desperation (I lost a staff member suddenly and I wanted to fill the position quickly) and I will be more aware to not do that in the future."

Ashley Farren – Ashley's Animal Academy, LLC
Downingtown, Pennsylvania

Action Steps – Hire and Manage Staff

Action Step

Set your timer for 15 minutes and answer this set of questions in your burnout recovery journal to decide if you need to hire (or hire more) staff:

- How do you react when a client calls or emails? Do you give each response the attention it deserves, or are you constantly juggling replies while taking care of other tasks?

- Have you ever lost a client because you simply did not have time for their needs? What happened? What would you have done differently if you'd had more time or more "hands on deck" in your business?

- How much of your time each week is spent on the long-term planning and vision of your business versus putting out "small fires"? Can you dedicate at least 20% of your work time to the visionary work that only you can do?

- When was the last time you took a day off? How about a week? When you are gone, who do you trust the most to handle any emergencies that arise?

Action Step

Make a list of two or three non-business tasks you would like to hire out and begin researching companies or individuals that can do each. Commit to calling or emailing one each day for a week so you can learn what pricing is for each in your area. Pick one at the end of the week and sign up for a one-time or trial opportunity.

Action Step

Figure out what tasks you can delegate to others with the following exercise:

In your burnout recovery journal, write down all tasks (personal and business) that you complete in a typical month and then organize them into three columns:

1. Items I'm willing to let go of/delegate

2. Items I might be willing to let go of/delegate

3. Items I am absolutely not willing to let go of/delegate

This will help you pinpoint what tasks are better suited for others and which you really do want to do yourself.

Action Step

Commit to delegating at least one responsibility this week. Follow the four steps in the "How Delegating Really Works" section of the chapter to choose the right task, the right person to delegate to and the right way to communicate what needs to be done. Add some time to your weekly or monthly schedule just for delegating. This will enable you to regularly assign new tasks and follow up on previous assignments.

Part Three

Bring Your Mind, Body and Spirit Back in Balance

"Feed your mind, body and spirit with nourishing thoughts, emotions and nutrients."

–Jennifer Bolus

NINE

Personalize Your Rest

Find the Best Way to Nurture YOU

*"Almost everything will work again if you unplug
it for a few minutes... including you."*

–Anne Lamott

Throughout this book so far, I have mentioned self-care, rest and nurturing yourself. The term "self-care" has become such an overused term that you may have heard it countless times without even knowing exactly what it means, or the term may no longer contain meaning for you due to its overuse. You might hear or read self-care suggestions like "take a nap" or "take a long bath" that don't sound appealing to you in the moment—or perhaps at all... so what do you do instead? I knew one woman who recharged by dancing to loud music—the louder and more intense the music, the better—and she often attended concerts when she needed to clear her head. (In fact, my husband is like this. He goes to concerts to, in his words, "floss his brain." After a deafeningly loud concert, he comes away renewed and refreshed from his brain flossing.) Personally, I crave solitude and silence to "fill my well" and restore my mind and spirit, so attending a concert is the last place I find inspiration or relief from stress!

This chapter will focus on why and how your nurturing and self-care will likely be completely different from someone else's and how to identify what refills *your* body, mind and spirit. Personalizing your rest and relief as you prevent and heal business burnout is more important than you may realize because making time for yourself is only part of the solution; knowing what to fill that new time *with* is the next essential piece.

Filling Your Own Personal Well

I mentioned "filling my well" in solitude and silence at the beginning of this chapter. This section will include a series of questions you can answer to better identify what helps restore and inspire you, so you will know how to refuel and recharge and what is most helpful for you to do with your self-care time you are working so diligently to carve out for yourself.

As part of this chapter's *Action Steps,* you will answer these questions in your burnout recovery journal. For now, simply read through them and start formulating ideas. As you do, pay special attention to any answers that come up more than once—those answers are likely your most powerful sources of rest and inspiration:

- List three of the most enjoyable hobbies you've had in your life so far. If none come to mind, think back to your childhood and what you enjoyed doing as a kid. Are you still doing any of them? If not, what is one simple action you can take today to explore one or more of these hobbies again?

- What passions have you neglected as you've built your business? (If nothing comes to mind, recall the story I shared earlier about my dream of extended travel after growing my business for years, and how that dream was buried so deep down that it took experiencing envy to reawaken that passion. You may find a similar buried passion or dream of your own.)

- Do you enjoy playing any sports? If you used to play a sport, but haven't recently, are there any recreational leagues in your area you could join?

- What inspired you to start your business? Writing a list of reasons you started your business and evaluating how many of those benefits you have achieved or are currently living can help you step back and remember your original goals, instead of getting stuck in day-to-day tasks.

- Does music have a profound effect on you? For some people, hearing or making music is one of the best forms of creativity

158

and catharsis. If so, what is your favorite song or genre? How does that music make you feel? When was the last time you heard, sang or played that music?

- What or where is your favorite place in the natural world? Have you ever had your breath taken away by a specific sunrise, sunset, waterfall, ocean or vista? When was the last time you visited that special spot? How did your body, mind and/or spirit feel when you were there?

- Do you have a favorite quote for times when you need a dose of inspiration? If so, write and post this quote somewhere you can see it regularly, such as your bathroom mirror or the dashboard of your car.

- What is something you have wanted to do but haven't yet tried? For example, do you wish you knew how to dance? Speak a new language? Cook gourmet meals? List two or three skills you want to learn.

- Where have you always wanted to travel but have not yet created the opportunity to visit?

As you can probably tell from reading these questions, some of your answers may be short and others may be in-depth and lengthy. If so, great! The goal of this chapter is to get you to think about—and recognize—your personal sources of inspiration and rest. These questions and answers will empower you to tap into your personal inspiration more often as you learn to nurture yourself, instead of only focusing on others and on your business.

In addition to the answers to the questions above, you may also find inspiration from the words of others. I have included a *Reading List* at the end of this book that contains books I read and found helpful in my own burnout recovery.

Burnout Recovery Tip

As you find books, articles and quotes that really speak to you, consider making your own essential reading list or quote board so you have a wellspring of inspiration when you need it.

Introverts vs. Extroverts (and Why It Matters)

Do you know if you are an introvert or an extrovert? Many people who think they know are actually the opposite of what they think because of common misconceptions about introverted and extroverted people. For example, not all introverts are shy, and extroverts are not always confident and outgoing. In truth, the difference lies in how you recharge and experience a sense of renewal: Introverts gain energy and renewal by having time alone. Extroverts recharge by spending time in the company of others. (Check the *Recommended Resources* section to find suggestions for helping you learn more about your introverted or extroverted tendencies.)

The difference really is that simple. If you are an introvert, you likely feel drained after a long period of socialization, even if you are naturally outgoing, enjoy connecting with people and had a great time. The woman I described earlier in the chapter, who uses concerts as a retreat, is actually an introvert (and so is my husband!). Although many people surround her at the concert, she goes alone and does not feel the need to talk to anyone there—the music is too loud to do any talking anyway! Even though the venue is often packed with concert goers, she finds mental solitude (or as my husband says, "brain flossing") in the music. Again, contrary to popular belief, being introverted does not always mean shy (although sometimes they do go together), but it does mean introverts need time alone to recover from a period of intense business demands or stress.

On the other hand, if you are an extrovert, you probably leave that same party, meeting or conference energized and eager to engage with more people or ready to tackle your next project. Extroverts are sometimes portrayed as loud individuals, who are always the life of the party and relish being in the limelight. But, as with stereotypes about introverts, these representations are also not always true. In reality, extroverts can be just as skilled at listening and working with others as introverts. The difference is that extroverts derive energy from social interaction with others, whereas introverts gain energy from solitude.

> INTROVERTS RECHARGE BY BEING ALONE. EXTROVERTS RECHARGE BY BEING WITH OTHERS.

You may be reading this section and wondering why it even matters if you are introverted or extroverted. What does any of this have to do with burnout anyway? The reason it matters is because knowing *how you most fully recharge* will enable you to make smarter and more intentional decisions in your burnout recovery.

If you are extroverted, you will probably want—or even need—to schedule regular interaction with a group of friends or colleagues. Pet care is often a solitary line of work, except for brief interactions with your human clients, so making a point to regularly initiate and schedule get-togethers with others will likely be an important part of your personal self-care routine. If you are introverted, you may need to do the complete opposite and carve out alone time in your schedule. Caring for pets does not usually "fill the well" for introverts, because although it is solitary, it's work, not self-care. I often hear from my coaching clients that they expect caring for pets will meet their need for interaction, but they are shocked and sad when it doesn't.

Depending on your family situation, carving out your essential solitude time may require more creativity to arrange than for others who don't have a spouse and/or children. I know many business owners who feel guilty taking time alone away from their spouse or children in addition to the time the business requires. I was one of those "guilty introverts" too, until I realized that alone time truly is the lifeblood of my creativity, and only when I've had alone time can I truly show up for others. The cherry on the sundae of awareness for me was realizing how crucial alone time is for my well-being. These realizations helped me get over the guilt of taking time for myself and perhaps it will help you get over it too. Being conscious and respectful of your introverted nature may give you the inner permission slip to schedule precious—and necessary—time to be alone. In fact, you will be more energized and present with your family *because* of that time alone. I know a woman with a very social job who specifically takes the longer commute route from work so that she can drive alone for a few more minutes before being with her family. She is much happier and more helpful (and as a result, more loving!) because of those few extra minutes of solitude that she gives herself.

Create Your Personal Oasis

Regardless of whether you're an introvert or an extrovert, creating your own personal, private place or special activity to recharge is as important as making a dedicated space for office work. Your personal oasis does not need to be large or even in your home. Whether you live in an apartment or on a sprawling homestead, it is important that you find a place or activity that refuels you. Many people find a personal retreat in daily exercise, and I've already mentioned others finding rest in music. Your personal oasis may be in your home, outdoors or in a favorite activity; what matters is that you designate an oasis for yourself so you can recharge.

You will need to do more than find a physical location for your self-care; you will also need to commit to setting aside the time for this personalized self-care. As you reset your schedule and your routines, be sure to carve out time for your personal retreat in your special spot. The idea of intentionally setting aside time and a location for your renewal and rejuvenation is not new. Author Brené Brown calls this space a clearing: *"Nothing calms me down like swimming. That's why, when I need to come back to myself, I grab my goggles and head for the pool. Maybe your clearing involves long walks at dusk, or maybe it's writing. Find an activity that centers you and then make time for it — no matter what."* Author Susan Caine borrows a term from Superman lore and refers to it as a "fortress of solitude." (Both of these authors' books can be found in the *Reading List* at the end of this book.) I've chosen the imagery of an oasis — a fertile area of life and energy in the middle of a desert.

This oasis will look different depending on your home, situation and personality. Your recharge oasis may be out in nature a few miles from your home. If so, set aside time weekly for a long hike or walk outside. You may set aside part of your home — a nook or corner of a room — and fill it with the items that can soothe or nurture you when you have downtime (books, music, beautiful furnishings, etc.). For others, this "place" of recharge is more an activity than an oasis: you may find energy or restoration in a fun or engaging hobby. In this case, you will probably want to create a budget and space in your home for this hobby. I had a client who said she found inspiration singing with a local choir, so she set aside time to attend weekly choir practice, even during her busy season at work.

Kristin's Story

In an earlier chapter, you read about—and if you completed the chapter activities, had your own experience with—active imagination. Another experience I had with active imagination involved determining how I could most fully recharge. I was feeling depleted by numerous projects, a recent move with my husband and lots of scheduled activities. I got still and quiet to figure out how I could most fully renew my spirit. What I saw when I got still and quiet and called my spirit in was shocking. I saw koi fish wiggling around on cement, gasping for air. I asked them what they needed, and one said, "We are like you, we are gasping for breath because we need water just like you need alone time. You are like us—a fish out of water. And not getting alone time is causing you to gasp for air, as surely as we are without water."

Whoa.

I quickly scheduled a retreat at a house in the woods, far away from people and the constant demands of my business and personal life. At the end of the retreat, when I checked in with the koi (who represented me) through active imagination, they were happily swimming in a large, clear and beautiful pond!

I have made it a point since that time to schedule at least a couple days away each month, if not more. In the occasional months where I really cannot find time to go away, I simply take myself out for a drive to a beautiful spot near the water or in the woods and relax in nature for a few hours.

Burnout Recovery Success Stories

"It was hard for me to figure out what would be most restorative for me. It seemed like whenever I would try and do something to decompress and truly focus on my mental health, something that could not be avoided in my work would arise, and I would have to step back in as the owner of the company, while all I had initially planned went by the wayside. I finally reached a point of burnout. I had to take a step back and re-evaluate what I wanted from my business. I restructured my business, added pet business software that literally cut all the hours of admin work in half, started using an accounting software and delegated more responsibility to my lead sitter. This has allowed more free time for myself and my family.

Now when I'm feeling depleted, I literally disconnect from everything. I make plans to do something fun, whether it's hiking with my hubby and dog pack or taking a much-needed trip somewhere my hubby and I have been wanting to go. I send a mass email letting my clients know I will not be able to be reached and provide them with my lead sitter's information. I try and do this at least once a month.

I am an introvert and I love being home most of the time. I do love hiking and being outdoors. I don't have a lot of interaction with others as I work from home. When I don't provide myself with self-care, stress starts to creep in. I become short-tempered and then realize I need a break.

I have two spots that are an oasis for me. Living in the mountains, we are surrounded by hiking. We enjoy the outdoors and all it has to offer. I also enjoy working out six days a week and this helps me get my mornings started right.

Being in business since 2007, I have learned a lot with trial and error. Personal care, resting and nurturing yourself should be at the top of each business owner's priority list. I have made this a priority for myself and it has really helped move my business in a more positive direction."
Julie Gonzalez – Faithful Friends Pet Sitting, LLC
Cary, North Carolina

"I am often 'on the go' and don't always notice how depleted I'm feeling until it's too late! It's at this point that I will take the time to leave my phone at home and walk through the woodland to the beach. I love to listen to the birds and the leaves blowing in the trees before taking in some sea air. On a calm day, I listen to the sound of the waves and feel relaxed, but I also love those really wild days where the waves crash against the shore and the wind whips up the spray; it's so refreshing. My oasis is the woodland that leads to the beach — as soon as I enter the trees, I feel myself completely let go of all my worries and feel like there is nothing to stress about. I always feel restored after one of these walks and then try to relax for the evening. A nice long bath finishes this off perfectly!

I often feel like I cannot switch off at home (probably because I work from home), so I often need to go somewhere in order to feel rested and restored.

It took me a very long time to realize that walks (especially with my dogs) really are the best way for me to personally nurture myself and feel rested and restored. I always thought I should do meditation, yoga, or sit and read a book but I tried all of these and they didn't help me. What I realized is that because I work from home, I often feel like there's work I should be doing and it's very hard to stop until it's done, I just can't switch off unless I physically take myself away from my home for a while.

I always thought I was an extrovert, so I was often going to parties and surrounding myself with a lot of people. However, in the last few years I realized that all this socializing leaves me feeling exhausted! Now I prefer to have a nice balance and time on my own to recuperate."

Kirsty Everard - Kirsty's Paws
Bournemouth, England

"How I nurture myself depends on the day, the time and the reason why I'm feeling depleted. Maybe I need to eat, maybe I need a nap, maybe I need some peace and quiet, maybe I need some energizing music, maybe I need to reshape my brain, maybe I need physical exercise, etc.

I've learned to listen to my body. It knows what it needs; I just have to listen! Some things I've done for as long as I can remember that are my regular self-care include journaling, art and reading. Doing activities I enjoy is a natural booster. My energy comes from things that give me excitement, so if I'm feeling depleted, I'm doing too many things that aren't bringing me joy in my life. Anytime I'm outside and/or around animals is a natural mood booster too!

I am definitely an introvert. I handle people best in small quantities. I've always been fine on my own and never 'needed' to be around people. I'd live quite happily as a hermit in the woods! Pets are my preferred company, even though I do have a significant other... it works out as he works a lot! Small doses of people work for me, but if I'm around too many people for too long, I get exhausted and cranky. I am not a go-go-go person, I like to ease into things (mostly) and think things over. So, reading and journaling and other similar quiet activities definitely make sense for me! I like hiking too and being in nature. It's good for my soul. Downtime is recharging and I need that. I like silence; too much noise puts me on edge and is distracting.

I wish I had more of an oasis but the closest I get is my office, which is the only area that's truly my space. I was able to set it up and decorate it however I wished, and it suits me. But I also love being outdoors. We have a little patio that I like to sit out on in the mornings."
Brienne Carey – BC Pet Care, LLC
Wheaton, Illinois

Action Steps – Personalize Your Rest

Action Step

Using the "Filling Your Own Personal Well" section of this chapter, answer the questions about inspiration in your burnout recovery journal. You may be surprised by the sources of inspiration and rest you discover in the process of answering those questions.

Then, pick at least one source of inspiration or self-care to focus on this week. Schedule any specific time you'd like to do this activity or experience in your weekly schedule and budget a reasonable amount for expenses (if needed).

Action Step

Make a list of quotes and songs you find inspiring in your burnout recovery journal. Then, use that list to make a quote board on Pinterest or an actual bulletin board in your office or home and playlist of motivational songs you can turn to when you need a jolt of inspiration. This quote board could hang in your office or be saved as a series of pictures on your phone. You might write out the quotes and hang them on your mirror or listen to your inspirational playlist when you drive to and from client homes. The goal of this *Action Step* is to have inspirational resources at the ready when you need a motivational push.

Action Step

Are you an introvert or an extrovert? If, after reading this chapter, you still aren't sure whether you recharge in solitude or in the company of others, take an online test by searching for "introvert/extrovert test" online or by using one of the resources in the *Recommended Resources* section. Use this information about yourself to make a list of three activities you can use to recharge when you feel overwhelmed, stressed or overworked.

Action Step

Identify your own personal oasis. You may need a physical location, a budget for supplies, a chunk of time in your schedule or all three. Whatever your oasis looks like, take the time today to set it up in your routine so that you can retreat there as needed.

TEN

Calm Your Mind and the Rest Will Follow

Use Mindfulness and Meditation to Mentally Recharge

*"You should sit in meditation for twenty minutes every day —
unless you're too busy; then you should sit for an hour."*

–Zen Proverb

Regular meditation is one of the single most powerful steps I took to recover from my own business burnout. Meditation allowed me time every day to reduce my stress and refocus my thoughts. A quick internet search reveals that I am not alone in this experience: Arianna Huffington, Jerry Seinfeld, Oprah Winfrey and former LinkedIn CEO Jeff Weiner have all listed regular meditation as helping them succeed in their busy professional lives.

In spite of all of these testimonials to the value of regular meditation, I still find some business owners skeptical of meditation and how it could be helpful for them. If you are approaching this chapter doubting that mindfulness and/or meditation can work for you, I encourage you to read the chapter with an open mind. You may also want to check the *Reading List* at the end of the book for the details on the book *Meditation for Fidgety Skeptics*, which does a wonderful job of explaining the science and process of meditation with meditation skeptics in mind.

Intentional Mindfulness (and How It Helps)

Mindfulness and meditation are often used interchangeably, although they are not exactly the same. I see the term "mindfulness meditation" a lot as well, which only adds to the confusion. Whereas mindfulness is a state of being, meditation is one of potentially many processes used to get to that state. One of my favorite ways to think about the difference comes from Ten Percent Happier, which was co-founded by Dan Harris, the author of the book I mentioned at the beginning of the chapter, *Meditation for Fidgety Skeptics*. The founders describe the relationship between mindfulness and meditation in terms of exercise: meditation is the workout or training you use to get to the strength or flexibility that is mindfulness.

Mindfulness is focusing on your present state and acknowledging your thoughts, feelings and physical sensations. It allows you to still your mind and be fully present and aware, instead of constantly multitasking and being two steps ahead of what is going on around you. Even if it is as simple as focusing on the sensations of a cup of tea or meal, rather than drinking or eating while thinking about or doing something else. Although there will be times when you need to reflect on the past or plan for the future, your quality of life (and the quality of your work) will likely improve when you focus more on the moment you are in. Instead of letting the past or the future dominate your mental space, intentionally focus on the present and commit to calmly, joyfully experiencing it.

Greg McKeown, author of the book *Essentialism*, said this: "Always-on culture is weird. It's not how humans thrive. It's not how productive people break through to the next level."

I completely agree! Not only is encouraging your mind to be still beneficial for your mental, emotional and physical health, it will likely help your business as well by enabling you to be productive instead of simply being busy. Because modern society and many of our cultures are so constantly in motion, it takes specific effort to stop the cycle of reaction and constant movement. If you have ever wanted to step back and catch your breath — and anyone reading a book about business burnout likely knows that feeling — cultivating and practicing mindfulness can help you learn to manage your emotions and feelings, instead of being in a constant state of reaction and impulse. When you're mindful, you can begin to cultivate a habit of responding rather than reacting, which is a powerful way to live life and run your business.

How to Use Meditation to Improve Your Mindfulness

If you are not in the regular practice of meditating, or if you would like to reboot your meditation practice, you may be wondering the best way to meditate. However, in the actual practice of meditation, there are as many different forms of meditation as there are locations from which to meditate! I have even known business owners who will meditate in their car between appointments. I recommend trying a few different variations and choosing the style and location that is most comfortable for you.

If you have never meditated before, or if regular meditation is not part of your routine, you may feel like you need to learn how to meditate before you get started. Don't let not knowing what to do be your excuse to avoid this helpful practice. It's very easy!

Here is a very basic meditation routine that works for many business owners because it is easy to do just about anywhere:

1. **Sit comfortably**. For many people, this may be in a chair instead of on the floor.

2. **Set a timer for five minutes.** In time, you may want to increase the time you spend on meditation to 15- or 30-minute sessions (or more), but for beginners, five minutes is plenty and a great starting point.

3. **Focus on your breathing.** It may help you to actually think "in" and "out" to yourself as you inhale and exhale deeply in order to keep your mind from wandering.

4. **Simply notice your thoughts as they pop up.** When your mind does wander (and it does for even experienced meditators), simply notice that you're thinking (thinking the word "thinking" when you notice yourself deep in thought can be helpful!), then take a deep inhale and exhale and bring yourself gently and nonjudgmentally back to the present moment by focusing on your breathing.

171

5. **End with a deep inhale and exhale.** When your timer rings, take one last deep breath and savor the feeling of stillness.

It really is that simple.

Many people enjoy guided (spoken) meditation, but it is not mandatory to have a guide, and in fact, some find guided meditation distracting. You'll find some suggestions in the *Recommended Resources* section at the end of the book if you would like to know more about guided meditation or recommendations for meditation apps that can help you cultivate a meditation practice.

> REGULAR MEDITATION IS GOOD FOR YOUR HEALTH, HAS BEEN SHOWN TO LOWER STRESS AND WILL HELP YOU ENJOY LIFE MORE FULLY.

I recently read a powerful book by Sarah Wilson: *First, We Make the Beast Beautiful,* which was a game changer for me. In the book, she talks about meditation and how she has been practicing meditation twice a day for 20 minutes a day for years, and even though she still doesn't feel like she does it "right," the benefits have been huge. If an experienced veteran of daily meditation still feels like she isn't getting it all right every time, there is no reason for you to feel insecure in your meditation routine. The point is to do it anyway—regular meditation is good for your health, has been shown to lower stress and will help you enjoy life more fully. Rather than getting hung up on needing or wanting to meditate perfectly, cultivate beginner's mind by simply doing it whenever, wherever and however you can.

Stop Information Overload

This chapter has been all about letting your mind settle in the present and rest in order to allow yourself a respite from the adrenaline and stress you probably feel during many workdays. Another aspect of mindful rest worth considering is the role of social media and online distraction in your mental state.

How much time do you spend on your phone, computer or social media each day? How much of that is related to business tasks? Have you ever gone online to post or read something specific, only to look up and realize how much time has passed (perhaps even hours!) without noticing? The rise of constant connectivity, thanks to modern technology, has left most of us overwhelmed with notifications, chirps, beeps and clamors for our attention. What is supposed to be a time-saving tool, like a phone or computer, can instead be a way to waste valuable time. We may be able to get tasks done faster than ever and communicate with people from all over the world, but many of us are lonely and lack meaningful leisure time because so much of our spare time is wasted online.

> **Burnout Recovery Tip**
> Use one or more of the apps in the **Recommended Resources** section for tracking how much time you spend online and to help you resist the constant distraction.

In order to combat this ever-present drive to be online, I suggest you consider a two-week social media fast. Think of this fast as putting your mind in a hammock and letting it rest at the end of the day. If two weeks feels too long to be offline, choose five days or even three days. Even a few days of exploring other ways to relax or unwind, instead of mindlessly scrolling through social media feeds, can help your mind reset.

For business-related social media, consider hiring a virtual assistant to monitor social media and/or schedule your posts in advance using an app like Hootsuite so you can completely disconnect except for when you are actively preparing business posts and updates. For personal use, there is no need to deactivate your accounts or make a grand announcement about leaving Facebook, Twitter, Reddit or any other social media site. Simply stop using them. Take the app off your phone if that's most helpful or move the app to a folder or separate screen so you don't see notifications every time you pick up your phone. In the first few days of trying to disconnect, you will probably find yourself reaching for your phone more often than you expected based on habit, but that habit will soon be replaced by other activities you enjoy more: reading, napping, fun hobbies, house projects or simply connecting with loved ones.

At the end of the social media fast, ask yourself the following questions:

1. Did my impulse to reach for my phone get less demanding during my time away?

2. Do I miss social media? If so, what did I miss about it?

3. Did anyone else notice that I wasn't online?

4. How was my sleep (both quality and quantity) during my social media break? Was it any different than the time before I started my social media break?

5. What did I find time to do during my time away from social media that surprised or delighted me?

Then, after careful consideration of the effects of your social media/distraction fast, decide which websites or activities to quit for good. When deciding how to move forward with media consumption, consider how your business will be impacted by your decision. You may experience reduced exposure or marketing (although using a virtual assistant or scheduled posts can help, as suggested earlier), but you may also find more time to focus on income-producing activities. When you do get ready to get back online, have a plan for what tasks you will do when you're logged on that site. Define a specific post you need to make or friend you want to follow up with, set a time limit for the activity (and use a timer to stay on track!) and then log off when you are done or the timer goes off. Learn to use social media as a tool instead of letting it drive you to distraction.

You may also want to consider scheduling dedicated times to be on the internet, similar to the way I recommended setting specific periods of time for responding to emails and voicemails earlier in the book. By doing so, you will limit your potential distractions and discover so much more time in your day for distraction-free work, income-producing activities or true rest and relaxation. Research has shown that the most productive work happens when periods of focused work are followed by complete rest. This concept of being "always on" or always available is exhausting, and that exhaustion is likely to degrade the quality of your work and prevent your mind from getting the rest and relaxation it needs to recharge and be ready to focus on your next important task.

Kristin's Story

I feel strongly that giving our minds space to rest is vital to being able to then see and make important life and business changes. Finding that space is harder now than ever before because of cell phones and our "always on" culture. It may be more difficult to rest the mind than it used to be, but it is even more important because of the constant demands for attention.

In the same way that cell phones can inhibit the mind from resting, I've also found that they can get in the way of true, heartfelt connection. Even something as benign as looking at tomorrow's weather on our phones can take us out of the present moment and away from each other — even if we're right next to each other.

Before I ever started my first business, I had an experience that taught me the true importance of paying attention to the moment I'm in instead of always looking ahead (or at my phone).

I was struggling to figure out what line of work to pursue, knowing I wanted work I would truly enjoy, since it would be something I would do for so many hours out of my day. One day, I was walking near my home and passed a woman walking two Golden Retrievers. She was wearing a shirt with a pet business name and phone number on it, so I asked her if she had a dog walking business. We spoke about her business for a moment and then she offered me a job. I took the job immediately and discovered, over the course of my time working for her, that I wanted to start my own pet care business.

I truly believe if cell phones had been around when I was walking that day, I might have missed the opportunity completely. I might have been looking at my phone or she might have been listening to a podcast or music on hers and not been available to talk. Without being present and aware, I might have missed one of the biggest callings of my lifetime!

This realization has led me to make a conscious effort to leave my phone in the car from time to time or when I'm at home and it's not needed, I put it away in a special box my husband and I have for phones, so I don't miss the opportunities in front of me. I encourage all couples and families to have a "cell phone box" in their home where the phones go at certain times so they can focus on each other, instead of being distracted by their phones and missing out on the moment.

Burnout Recovery Success Stories

"I practice meditation. I have one guided meditation I follow that allows me to dive into my hopes and dreams and helps me visualize different things in my life. It goes into such great detail that I can visualize it so thoroughly that I can practically feel, see and smell it! While I may not be at the 'final picture,' I am well on my way. Some of it, I had no idea I wanted until practicing meditation.

Meditation is handy to reduce my stress level, and therefore it improves my overall mood. And my mood affects everything! Yoga is nice for that too — or really any form of exercise. Movement keeps me in a more relaxed state and helps settle my brain, which in turn keeps me calm and better able to deal with anything that comes along. Keeping positive is key to making anything and everything easier to deal with! Focusing on the present is also key. If I'm thinking about all the other things I need to do that day, then all I do is add unnecessary stress, which also tends to make me more forgetful. Being mindful about the present moment keeps me focused on what's happening right now, which keeps me calm and centered."
Brienne Carey – BC Pet Care, LLC
Wheaton, Illinois

"Let me preface this by saying I am not a consistent or a regular church-goer by any stretch of the imagination. That said, I am Episcopal and love the peaceful quiet meditation-like feel of the early morning services, with the smell of old wood from the Gothic church. Early 7am Sunday mass has few people and no singing, so I can have my thoughts to myself.

I have also studied self-hypnosis from a hypnotherapist and practice the tools I have learned in my daily life. I use controlled breathing, white noise and clearing of the mind from head to toe to help me sleep. It helps release the muscle tightness that I don't realize I have until I take inventory of myself. I took this self-hypnosis program many years ago and practice this when I am feeling restless."
Amy Sparrow – Furkid Sitting & Services, LLC
Baton Rouge, Louisiana

"Meditation is a huge part of my life! In order for me to have peace of mind, it's important for me to meditate consistently every single day. I can greatly feel the effects of it when I don't. When I meditate, I often feel happy, joyous and free. When I don't, I often feel irritable, discontent and full of fear. When I consistently meditate, I have a clear head. I'm more enjoyable to be around. I'm definitely more organized and more productive. I can focus so much better. When I meditate consistently, I don't react to life out of fear. I'm able to pause before reacting to something. Better yet, I respond to life instead of reacting to it. I have heard others say that praying is talking to God and meditating is listening. I like that."
Michelle Sabia – Paws & Claws Pet Sitting Services
Cave Creek, Arizona and Litchfield, Connecticut

Action Steps – Calm Your Mind and the Rest Will Follow

Action Step

Give yourself permission to not be "on" all the time and give your mind space and time to rest. For example, intentionally savor your morning coffee or other beverage. Even if you have important actions you need to take in your business or personal life, allow your mind at least a few minutes to rest today. For some, this process may be easy, and if so, you will be ready to move on to the next *Action Step* quickly. For others, you may need to spend some time today learning more about the benefits of mindfulness and meditation before you are ready to fully commit to adding both to your routine. Check the *Recommended Resources* section and *Reading List* at the end of this book for suggestions on where to get information to learn more about mindfulness and meditation.

Action Step

Meditate for a minimum of five minutes every morning for two weeks using the simple meditation described in this chapter, a guided meditation app or any other meditation style you prefer. At the end of the two weeks, write in your burnout recovery journal any benefits or effects you've noticed due to the meditation. You can find information about meditation apps in the *Recommended Resources* section.

Action Step

In your burnout recovery journal, write a short list of what you could do with the time you currently spend online or on social media. When there is a void of time or focus, it will want to be filled by something, so choose what to fill it with before you move on to the next *Action Step*.

Action Step

Take a break from social media and other internet distractions for a social media fast for three or five days, or, if you feel brave, a full two weeks. If even three days feels too long, you can start with 24 hours. At the end of the time period you've chosen, answer the five questions listed in the "Stop Information Overload" section of this chapter in your burnout recovery journal.

Action Step

As was suggested with responding to voicemails and emails, schedule one or two periods of time each day (or less often, if you can) for checking and responding to social media notifications, emails and other messages. Find a friend or family member you can tell about your new online hours as a way to commit to keeping that schedule and so you have accountability if you are tempted to get online outside of those times. Bookend them at the beginning and end of every day of your social media fast.

ELEVEN

Reclaim Your Morning

The Unexpected "Secret Sauce" for Clarity in Business and Life

"When I'm tempted to skip my morning routine or another form of self-care, I remind myself that I can better serve the people I love and the projects I care about when I start with me."
-Courtney Carver

How you start your morning sets the tone for everything else that will follow that day. Even if you are not a morning person or are more productive in the evening, the first few hours of each day can still be the most important in determining whether the day will go according to plan. In this chapter, I will describe my own morning routine—and how my routine helps me combat my own burnout—and give you tips for designing your own personalized morning. If you have never given much thought to what you do first each day, this chapter may be one of the most important you will read in this book. If you already have a morning routine you feel is working for you, read on anyway— you may find suggestions or ideas that can help you improve your current routine.

How My Morning Routine Changed My Business and Personal Life

In the early days of running my pet care business, I would often jump out of bed and immediately check client messages. Because I went from asleep to "business mode" in a matter of minutes, nearly every waking moment of each day was spent addressing my clients' needs. One day, in the midst of my own burnout, I realized I needed to dedicate some time just for me every morning. Not only did I need this time before I was caring for my clients, I needed this time before I was taking care of *anyone else*, including my own pets or loved ones.

When I first made the decision to carve out a morning routine for myself, I wondered where I would find the time. Dedicating even 30 minutes when I had so much other work to do felt extravagant, and I worried that my business would suffer or that I would be too stressed about the day's work to really make the most of my morning. Once I tried out my morning routine, I decided to commit to this daily ritual. My workdays were regularly filled with a peace and solidity they'd never had before. Like many of the other suggestions in this book, creating and implementing a morning routine not only made me healthier and happier, but it also improved my business. As a result, I was calmer, more grounded and able to make better decisions throughout the whole day.

> **Burnout Recovery Tip:**
> "I find that checking my phone in the morning tramples over my positive vibes, because we all know that checking messages is like rattling a wasp nest."
> –Stephanie Lee

My morning routine is now part of my daily work schedule. I can't imagine starting a day without my personal morning time anymore — in fact, when I do start the day without my morning routine, I often feel lost, like an unmoored boat. I use this precious and sacred time to connect with and ground myself before my time and attention are pulled outward and focused on others.

Set Up a "Win" Every Day

When you think about an ideal morning routine, what comes to mind? If you're imagining an elaborate schedule (and wondering how in the world to make it work in your actual life), you may be surprised at how simple the morning routines of many successful business owners and entrepreneurs are.

The way Tim Ferriss, author of *The Four-Hour Workweek*, describes his morning routine is helpful when trying to figure out how to spend your first few hours each day. He has a list of five items to accomplish each morning. If he gets at least three done, he considers the day a win. He gives himself only five morning tasks and is satisfied with only three. He says he intentionally sets the bar low so that he can start every day with a win and have control over a few things completely in his power. (In case you're curious, his five things are (1) make the bed, (2) meditate, (3) do five to ten reps of some exercise, (4) make tea and (5) write five to ten minutes of morning pages or journaling.)

I have made an informal study of the morning routines of highly effective business owners and entrepreneurs, and most routines are surprisingly simple and consistent—the common thread between most is choosing a few essentials and sticking to them every day.

> STARTING EACH DAY ENERGIZED IN MIND AND NOURISHED IN SPIRIT WILL BE AN INTEGRAL PART OF HEALING AND PREVENTING BURNOUT.

Allowing yourself the gift of a simple morning routine, so you start each day energized in mind and nourished in spirit, will be an integral part of healing and preventing burnout. Each day's routine can be an opportunity to "check in" with yourself and readjust if you've gotten too far off center.

Design Your Ideal Morning Routine

Every morning routine looks a little different because of the differences in each person's needs and situation. For example, if your morning responsibilities include taking children to school, you may have to start your routine earlier in the day or divide your morning routine into two parts—steps you can take before the school run and those you complete after. On the other hand, pet professionals whose busiest time of day is the afternoon or evening may have more uninterrupted time later in the morning.

As you plan your own morning routine, which you will do in this chapter's *Action Steps*, keep the following in mind:

1. **Start the night before.**

   A successful morning routine actually starts the night before. Each evening when I finish my work, I do a quick office cleanup and write down my to-do list for the following day, so I start each day with a clean, organized workspace. Other preparations to consider include making sure you have everything you need for breakfast, laying out your gym clothes (if you will start the day with a workout) and writing out your plan for the morning, especially at times when you are starting or modifying your morning routine. By giving yourself a written routine, you won't need to remember what you plan to include in the routine — it will all be written out for you.

2. **Wake up at the same time every day.**
   Research has shown that waking up at the same time every day makes it easier to wake up and keeps your body's natural rhythms in sync. Even if your schedule changes from day to day, choose a time to wake up that you can stick to every day — even on your day off. In Chapter Fifteen, I will give you more suggestions on how to set this habit and easy ways to wake up even if you are not naturally a morning person.

3. **Include journaling or other reflection time.**
   One of the most significant changes I made to my morning routine was to start writing Morning Pages. The idea for these Morning Pages came from a book about creativity, *The Artist's Way* by Julia Cameron.

   The concept of Morning Pages is simple: Each morning, write for three pages about whatever is on your mind that day. Don't edit or worry about spelling and grammar as you write. You may even choose to not go back and read your pages later. These pages are an opportunity to think and process as you start each morning, to clear your mind from anything that might pull your focus away from the day ahead.

   I find my Morning Pages help me process frustrations as well as direct my attention to needs and ideas I might have otherwise ignored without the dedicated time set aside to simply write and reflect.

4. **Get moving.**
   I'll write more about the importance of exercise and movement in preventing burnout in a later chapter, but plan on starting each day with some movement. Even if your actual workout or exercise comes later in the day, add a small amount of

movement to your morning routine to wake up your brain and get your blood pumping. In the example I gave earlier, Tim Ferriss includes as few as five repetitions of some exercise each morning. It could be as quick as five push-ups or squats — even just a few minutes of movement can help you reap the rewards of better focus and energy throughout the day.

5. **Make adjustments as needed.**

A morning routine does not have to be fixed or rigid. Your routine will likely need adjusting over time as you and your life change. Changes in health, demands on your time, family needs or your personal interests will probably require you to modify your morning routine occasionally. Remember, the goal is to design a morning routine that infuses your day with energy and peace instead of overwhelm. It's unlikely any two pet professionals will have the same morning routine as one another, nor would they need to. Your ideal morning routine will probably be an ongoing work in progress as you discover what works for you and what does not.

Tips for Better Journaling

I've already mentioned journaling or writing Morning Pages as part of your morning routine because of how powerful the process can be, especially considering it is such a simple action with the potential for a big return on your time investment.

If you are reading this and thinking you are not a journal writer or that Morning Pages don't seem like they'll work for you, I encourage you to try writing each day for three weeks before you disregard the suggestion entirely. I've given this same three-week Morning Pages advice to coaching clients who are skeptical about how writing in a journal can help their business. The clients who are the most resistant *nearly always* come back to tell me how much more peaceful, focused and productive they are after just a few weeks of writing Morning Pages. From their experiences and my own, I am confident you will probably discover a similar benefit.

Whether you are journaling for the first time or want to make the most of your current daily writing time, here are three tips for better journaling:

1. **Write whatever comes to mind in the moment, without judging it or editing it.**

   You may find yourself writing about events in the past, dreams and goals for the future or simply pressing concerns with a client. Every day's writing might be different, but don't let the lack of a theme stop you from writing. This is a time to write whatever comes to mind in the moment you are in, no planning or preparation necessary.

2. **Be honest.**

   These pages are not for anyone else. Many times, you may not even read them again. Complete honesty can be difficult, especially when writing about mistakes you have made or challenges you're experiencing, but the honesty you bring to your journal will allow you to truly process what you are writing about. You may find yourself writing about feelings you're having toward a family member or friend, a client that is causing you concern, a big tip you got from a client or something you're excited or happy about. Anything that's on your heart and mind is welcome on the pages.

3. **Keep writing.**

   Don't let writer's block keep you from journaling. If you run out of ideas, close your eyes and re-center yourself, then keep the pen moving. You may be surprised at how much more you have to say than you originally thought.

I have been writing Morning Pages *nearly every day* since 1990. The most helpful part of Morning Pages for me has been the transformation of what I start writing about on the first page of the day compared to what I'm writing about by page three. As I write about whatever is interesting to me or bothering me on a given day, I often find myself finishing up with a great business idea or realizing who I need to talk to next about a particular venture. My creativity is unlocked in the process of writing, which has led me to tap into, and move forward with, many of my best ideas.

Kristin's Story

Many years ago, when I first started writing Morning Pages, I had no idea writing in my journal would become one of my "secret weapons" in business, but it has. The reason why is this: I am able to process life and business challenges on a daily basis as they come. At the same time, I am often able to come up with solutions to those challenges. Not only that, but even though I usually write my to-do list the night before, I will often get crystal clear during my journal writing about what is most important to focus on that day, as well as come up with other tasks I hadn't previously thought of the night before. I also believe my intuition/gut instinct has been sharpened and honed due to connecting with myself during my writing every day. It's rare that I'll go a few days without journal writing, but I notice when I do; I feel more than a bit unmoored and lost without the writing to steady me. It's helped me step into my True North and I realize today that writing Morning Pages is my most important self-care item. If I've got limited time, journaling is the most important action I take to get me started on the right foot and facing in the right direction in the morning.

When I first got married, I found myself wondering if Morning Pages were still important because they were often hard to do in the morning (morning is my husband's favorite time to connect with me). When I found myself going days without journaling, I realized I needed to make my Morning Pages a top priority, along with my morning time with my husband. Now, I will spend quality time with my husband upon first waking up, and after a few minutes, I let him know it's time for my journaling. At that point, I move to our guest room or some other private spot in our home.

Even after a few years of this schedule, my beloved husband will sometimes complain about me leaving him and our special morning time together to then go write in my journal. When this happens, I remind him that my writing enables me to step into who I truly am each day and the work I'm doing in the world, as well as to be there more fully for him and myself throughout the day. It was much easier to have a morning routine before I was married, but I was lonely before I was married! Now I'm learning how to both take care of myself and give our relationship quality time—it's not always an easy process, but when we live with other humans, it's a necessary skill!

Burnout Recovery Success Stories

"My most productive time is early in the morning. I let one of my dogs out at 5:30 am and feed her. Then I go back into bed with the other dog and read my emails to see if anything pressing has come into my emails overnight. I handle anything time sensitive right then. I then read the news and do the rest of my morning routine followed by breakfast, coffee and work about 9am. By the time my other dog gets out of bed at about 10am, I'm already into my work routine."

Amy Sparrow – Furkid Sitting & Services, LLC
Baton Rouge, Louisiana

"I am always at my best in the morning. I can get more done in those first few hours than I seem to manage at any other time of day!

My typical morning routine is I check my emails right after I get up and then make a cup of tea. While I am on my first cup, I plan what action I need to take and send off replies. This morning time is a really productive time for me and by my second cup of tea, I am well into my to-do list. I usually get quite a lot done even before my dog wakes up for breakfast.

If I don't use my morning productively, I feel lost for the rest of the day, I start to do too many things at once to try and get them all done, and it never goes to plan because something else always comes up!"

Kirsty Everard – Kirsty's Paws
Bournemouth, United Kingdom

"I hate mornings. My idea of hell is waking up to an alarm clock. I am most productive from the time it gets dark outside until 3 or 4am. I can't really keep these hours though because there's almost always something I need to do before noon the next day and I also need 8-9 hours of sleep to feel human. It's a work in progress!"

Shelly Ross – Tales of the Kitty
San Francisco, California

"In the morning, I get up, I eat breakfast, and then I get dressed right away. Getting out of pj's as soon as possible gets me out of 'lazy mode.' I take the dog out, then I either do visits or I head straight to the computer and get

those things taken care of immediately. Then the rest of the day is mine to do whatever else. I like getting the necessary things that need to be done out of the way so I can relax and go with the flow the rest of the day."
Brienne Carey – BC Pet Care, LLC
Wheaton, Illinois

Action Steps – Reclaim Your Morning

Action Step

Using the suggestions and examples in this chapter, as well as the "Design Your Ideal Morning Routine" section, create a sample morning routine. If you already have a routine in place, use the chapter to refine your routine further.

Then, write out your routine and post it in a place where you will see it each morning.

Action Step

For the next three weeks, commit to writing your own Morning Pages every day. Remember the suggestions from the chapter: (1) write about whatever comes to mind, (2) be honest and (3) keep writing.

At the end of the three weeks, look back and ask yourself the following questions:

1. What have I learned about myself and my business in the course of writing Morning Pages for three weeks?

2. What (if anything) has surprised me in the process?

3. What would I tell a friend or fellow business owner who asks why I write Morning Pages?

Action Step

Commit to a morning routine every day for three weeks. It is okay if your routine is not a perfect fit at first. At the end of the first week, evaluate your routine and determine what is working and what needs to change. Then, modify your routine as needed. Do the same sort of evaluation again at the end of three weeks. If you need further ideas, inspiration or guidance, check out the *Recommended Resources* and *Reading List* for morning routine inspiration.

TWELVE

Renewal Through Retreats and Vacations

Give Yourself Regular, Scheduled Time Off to Prevent Burnout

"A field that has rested gives a bountiful crop."

–Ovid

When was the last time you took a vacation from your business? If you are like many pet professionals, the answer is likely *too long ago!* Taking intentional breaks away from work to relax and recharge is good for all of us, but especially for small business owners and entrepreneurs. When you are in charge of running a business, especially a service-oriented business, taking time off is essential for preserving your internal balance and peace.

My Vacation Affirmation

As I shared earlier in the book, I discovered many years ago how regular vacations actually improved my business — in addition to the many personal benefits. In fact, it became a mantra of mine: *The more vacations I take, the more money I make!* Not only do I usually make more money when I commit to regular vacations, I also feel

> TAKING TIME OFF IS ESSENTIAL FOR PRESERVING YOUR INTERNAL BALANCE AND PEACE, ESPECIALLY AS A SERVICE-BASED BUSINESS OWNER.

more grounded and ready to handle the ups and downs of my personal and professional life when I return.

Although it took a great leap of faith to step away from my business the first time I traveled for an extended period of time, getting away for short or long trips on a regular basis has now become a habit. When I saw that my business could not only survive without me but was thriving, I established a regular pattern of living in Bali for a few months at a time. I was surprised to discover that I even made more money by not actively working than I ever had while I was working! Since that time, I have continued to travel with my husband to locations around the world for extended periods of time. Although my vacations require more coordination since getting married because my husband is not self-employed, these times away are a regular and favorite part of every year.

The Benefits of Regular Vacation Time

The benefits of regular vacations and retreats are numerous and well documented. As this is a book devoted to curing and preventing burnout for pet professionals, I will focus specifically on the burnout-preventing benefits.

Of the many reasons to take regular vacations, here are four:

1. **Vacations give you the chance to focus on the big picture.**
   I often come back from a vacation or retreat with new ideas for my business ventures. A new perspective comes with taking a step back from the day-to-day work of my business, and I have heard similar comments from many of my coaching clients. Many times, the solution to a complex issue will become clear when you give yourself time, space and the chance to look at the problem from a distance. Vacations can often be the vehicle to provide that perspective.

2. **Your body will have a chance to rest.**
   Even if you are diligent about office hours and a good night's sleep, the reality of running a service-based business is that long hours and intense efforts are sometimes unavoidable. Giving yourself permission to completely disconnect from work and truly rest can often improve your health, energy and focus.

3. **You will be more productive when you get back.**
   Taking time for a vacation or retreat after a big project or busy season is a great way to recover and find your balance once

more, but taking a vacation or a retreat *before* a similarly stressful time can be equally important. Most coaching clients report feeling more focused and energized about their businesses after a vacation. If your burnout is causing you to dread or resent work, you may be past due for some time away.

4. **Your staff members will have a chance to shine.**
   It can be nerve-racking to take an extended vacation and leave an office manager or other staff member in charge for the first time. On the other hand, there is no better way to demonstrate your commitment to delegation than regular, scheduled vacations where you leave the business in the capable hands of others. Your team members will respond to your trust and more often than not, prove they are worthy of it. You may come back from your vacation with a clearer idea of which staff members are the most valuable to your business and which (if any) may not be a good fit.

Despite the many benefits of time off for small business owners and entrepreneurs, a study by Sage North America shows that small business owners are actually taking *less* time off than they were a few years ago. Now that you have a better idea of the benefits of vacation on your health, your peace of mind and your business, the next question is how to find the time.

Burnout Recovery Tip
Plan a regular weekly date night with your partner, with friends or with yourself. Commit to go, especially if you are tired and don't want to go when the time comes. Nine times out of ten, you will likely be happy you went anyway.

Finding the Time and Money for Vacation

In earlier chapters, I pointed out how your budget and time plan are conscious, actionable reflections of your top priorities. Finding time and money for a vacation is no different; if a vacation is important enough to you, you can find the time. No, you may not be able to travel for two months this year, but you can start taking more time off than you have previously by making your vacation time a mandatory budget and schedule item.

How often should you get away? The answer likely depends on your business — how long you've been in business, how much staffing help you have and where you are in the business growth process. As a general rule, I recommend you take time off every month, even if it is just a single day off (or if that feels like too much, a half day) to start.

Sometimes, when we're burned out, we make excuses to avoid doing the very things that will restore and renew us. Going away on vacations and to enjoy quality time with family and friends is often an antidote to burnout.

In addition to taking a half or full day off each month, I also suggest you take a full week off every year at the very least, so you have time to truly rest and reconnect with life away from your business self. Rather than focusing on the bare minimum, I encourage you to start planning now for your dream vacation. How much time off would you take every year if you knew your business would thrive in your absence? It may be some time before you can confidently take your dream vacation, but by stating your ideal now, you will have taken the first step toward making it a reality.

What Makes a Restful Retreat

Another equally important aspect of taking vacations to prevent and heal burnout is to identify what makes for a restful retreat for you. A week-long road trip and family reunion may be important and worthwhile, but it may not be restorative or restful. In Chapter Nine, I wrote about finding the best way to nurture yourself based on your interests, inclinations and personality. Think back to the work you did in that chapter or flip back to the chapter now for a refresher. An ideal, restful retreat for an introvert is likely very different than for an extrovert. Knowing yourself and what you most need will be important when choosing how to spend your precious vacation time.

While some vacations can — and should — be just for fun or for connecting with loved ones, commit to giving yourself some time for rest and reflection as well. While running Microsoft, Bill Gates famously took an entire week off twice a year to be by himself in a cabin to do nothing but read, rest and think. He credits those "think weeks" with some of his best ideas.

While your ideal retreat will not be the same as anyone else's, look for the following when planning your own "think week" (or weekend, or day):

- **A place to be alone.**
  Whether it's a cabin in the woods or just a private hotel room, find a place you can be alone when you need time and space to think, reflect and relax.

- **Time to disconnect.**
  I encourage you to leave your phone and computer at home when you go on a restful retreat, or at the very least, put technology away except for certain times a day when you check messages and make calls. The more time you give your mind to disconnect from always being on, the more restful your retreat will be.

- **Beautiful surroundings that feed your soul.**
  Many people find time outdoors grounds them in a way that nothing indoors can. Time spent in the woods, on a hike, at the beach or simply out in nature can feed your soul if you are one of these people. For others, experiencing beautiful art, stirring music or dance leaves them energized and inspired. When you plan your ideal retreat, keep in mind what sort of environment meets your deepest needs.

In time and with practice, you will find your own perfect retreat. If you need ideas of where to start, do some research on sites like Airbnb, VRBO and Hotel Tonight so you can quickly decide where to go when you are ready for a retreat.

Kristin's Story

As I mentioned in an earlier chapter, I am someone who needs regular time in solitude to come back to myself and my center. A few years ago, I scheduled a few days on my own and stayed at a house in the woods in Big Sur. I found it to be exactly what I needed! Now, this retreat is a regular part of my month, and I often book many months in advance so it's on my calendar and I can plan my work and personal life around that time. I also go there for regular "work retreats," which you'll read more about in a coming chapter. I have enjoyed going to other vacation homes on Airbnb for a solo retreat, but I have found having a regular, familiar place that I know and love, like the Big Sur house, works best for me. Once I found a location with my most important qualities (quiet and surrounded by nature) where I can go to rest and experience renewal on an ongoing basis, I stuck with it.

Burnout Recovery Success Stories

"My vacations are planned a year in advance. I take full advantage of my credit card points and travel to the mainland where we store our RV. I put all business expenses on the credit card and get to fly free at least three times a year with my family of four. I pay my credit card off in full every month – and have been doing so for the last eight years – thus no interest charge.

My staff always knows well in advance, and I start preparations to leave two weeks in advance. I think preparation is the key. My list usually includes ordering supplies, paying all bills, getting banking and payroll done, meeting with staff/managers and making sure I have access to my software programs wherever I am."
Karen Furtado – Shear Magic Pet Salon
Hilo, Hawaii

"I have come to learn how very important vacations are as a pet sitter and business owner, even though they can definitely be a challenge to plan and stick to! I typically have at least one big vacation planned every year for about two weeks to visit friends and family in Connecticut, where I'm from. Then, I like to sprinkle a lot of little trips throughout the year, even if it's just a quick day trip to get out of town and away from business. I think of it like how parents need a break from their children. Obviously, parents love their children so much and hate to leave them, but they are better parents when they get that break away from their children. For me, what has made this possible is having great staff who are properly trained and having a team I can trust to take care of my business while I'm away. Giving up control of my business has been so hard to do, but the reward I get from being able to take a vacation because of that letting go of control is priceless. My business is so much better off when I take regular vacations!"
Michelle Sabia – Paws & Claws Pet Sitting Services
Cave Creek, Arizona and Litchfield, Connecticut

"I take time off on a regular basis. I usually plan to have a set weekend off every other month. That way, my clients know exactly when I will be away, and they can work around my vacation schedule. I try to plan time off in advance by giving my clients at least one- or two-months' notice. I often look back at previous years' schedules and estimate when a quieter time may be to take my vacation. It's worked out well. I fortunately have excellent clients who understand I need to live my life too and are very understanding and accommodating as I am for them. Most of my vacations are to go back home and visit family as we live in separate states. I try to do that once or twice a year for two to three days each time. I also try to take one longer vacation from four to seven days. My boyfriend and I have similar busy schedules and we rarely take vacation or time off in 'nice' weather as that's when both of us are the busiest with work. We usually aim for our vacation to be sometime between November and February, which is generally the quieter time for both of us."

Brienne Carey – BC Pet Care, LLC
Wheaton, Illinois

Action Steps – Renewal Through Retreats and Vacations

Action Step

What benefits have you seen from prior vacations, retreats or breaks you have taken from your business? Make a list in your burnout recovery journal of all the positives you've experienced when you take time off. Then, go back to "The Benefits of Regular Vacation Time" section and add any benefits you would like to experience in your journal. These lists will be your inspiration and motivation to do the work of preparing for and committing to time off.

Action Step

Budget for a weekly or monthly mini retreat or vacation and/or date night in both your time plan and your financial budget. Then, contact anyone you want to take with you and choose a date. Put it on your calendar and commit to going, even if you are tired or worn out. Remember, connection with loved ones is often the antidote to burnout!

Action Step

Plan a trip in which you will be away from your business for at least a week. If you haven't taken more than a day off before, your week trip may be next year sometime; or, if you are more accustomed to taking time off, schedule it for sooner rather than later. Once you have a date selected, notify your staff and clients (if applicable) and get everyone prepared for your time off.

Action Step

What makes a restful retreat for you? Using the bullet points in the "What Makes a Restful Retreat" section, identify any must-haves or deal breakers for retreats for you. Use this list to find your own retreat for a "think week" of your own by comparing what you're looking for to what is offered when you evaluate possible retreats.

Part Four

Partner with Your Body to Recover from Burnout

"For fast-acting relief, try slowing down."

–Lily Tomlin

Prevent the Physical Price of Burnout

Treat Your Body with the Care It Deserves

"Burnout occurs when your body and mind can no longer keep up with the tasks you demand of them."

–Del Suggs

Burnout — whether from the stress of running a business or another cause — is often more than a mental and emotional problem. Extended periods of stress and depletion can also have a negative impact on your physical health. In addition to the steps outlined so far in this book, healing and preventing burnout will probably also require partnering with your body to address your physical symptoms and warning signs you may be receiving.

At the end of this chapter, you will read stories from other pet professionals who have experienced the physical price of burnout firsthand. As you read this chapter and then read their personal experiences, you will find suggestions for protecting your most precious gift — your health.

The Physical Signs of Burnout

While every reaction or symptom of burnout may be different for each person, there are some common signs and symptoms you may experience if you are feeling burned out. You can read through a list of more general burnout signs in the Introduction. There are also documented and recognized physical symptoms of burnout and stress, some of which are obvious and others which may seem more unexpected.

Read through this list of some physical symptoms of burnout and stress and see how many apply to you:

1. **Elevated heart rate.**
    When you experience sudden stress, like swerving to avoid an accident, your body floods with adrenaline and cortisol. Your heart naturally starts pumping faster in order to spread these hormones through the body more quickly. Without these physical reactions, you would not have the reflexes needed to respond to sudden changes or dangers. Your body is not designed to experience this stressed state for long, however. Long-term stress, like the overwhelm and anxiety that accompanies burnout, may prevent the body from quickly returning back to normal after stressful events. This constant stress can damage your cardiovascular system and increase your risk of high blood pressure, stroke or heart attack.

2. **Digestive and gut problems.**
    For some people, stress and anxiety are often accompanied by stomach aches or other stomach issues. Even if you don't notice any stomach pain when you are stressed, it is likely taking a toll on your digestive system anyway. Acid reflux, constipation, irritable bowel syndrome and changes in gut bacteria are symptoms of stress you may have assumed are only related to what you ate instead of the price of burnout on your body.

3. **Skin and hair problems.**
    If you already deal with a skin condition such as eczema or psoriasis, elevated stress levels are likely to make the issue worse. Being under stress for long periods of time has also been shown to lead to hair loss, hives and unexplained rashes — even in people without a history of skin problems.

4. **Difficulty sleeping.**
    Chapter Fifteen is dedicated entirely to the reasons sleep is essential for healing and preventing burnout, so all I will mention here is the way stress affects your sleep patterns. If you are unable to fall asleep or stay asleep, stress and burnout may be the cause. Even though you likely feel more exhausted

and drained than normal when you are burned out, insomnia is a common symptom of stress. Not everyone experiences trouble sleeping when they are burned out, but people under intense or prolonged stress who already suffer from anxiety are at an even higher risk than normal to develop insomnia.

5. **Shoulder, neck, back and jaw pain.**
Stress might be responsible for muscle soreness, tightness or spasms. Tension headaches, knots in your shoulders and jaw pain are also often the result of stress. In severe cases, stress can even lead to temporomandibular joint (also known as TMJ) disorders in the jaw.

6. **Weakened immune system.**
One of the most problematic physical symptoms of burnout is a weakened immune system. When you experience long-term stress, you are more likely to catch a cold or the flu. In serious cases, stress can also lead to autoimmune disorders or make existing autoimmune issues worse.

7. **Reduced sex drive and reproductive problems.**
When you're stressed, it's not just that you are too tired to think about romance. In many cases, reduced sex drive and reproductive disorders are actually symptoms of stress. In women, burnout and chronic stress can lead to irregular cycles, lowered sex drive and difficulty getting pregnant. In men, stress can interfere with testosterone production, sex drive and normal reproductive functions.

While burnout and stress affect every individual differently, you have likely noticed at least some of these symptoms if you are experiencing burnout. Dealing with stress and burnout on an ongoing basis can lead to a dangerous cycle, as physical problems and illness make it even more difficult to address the causes of burnout.

Burnout Recovery Tip
If you notice any new or concerning symptoms of burnout, consult with a physician about what you are experiencing. Recovering from burnout will often help you feel better. Similarly, feeling better will also make it easier to heal from — and prevent — burnout.

FEAR: Feel Everything and Recover

As I mentioned when talking about negative beliefs, it is very common for business owners to power through times of exhaustion and stress. Putting your physical needs on the back burner and just focusing on the needs of others (and your business), is not the way to heal and preserve your health.

Business guru Zig Ziglar is credited with saying this about fear: *"F-E-A-R has two meanings: 'Forget Everything and Run' or 'Face Everything and Rise.' The choice is yours."* When it comes to physical health, FEAR can also stand for "Feel Everything and Recover." It's counterintuitive to want to be in your body when you're stressed or burned out and overwhelmed, but simply feeling is one of the keys to recovery. Instead of pushing down your symptoms or ignoring what your body is trying to tell you, let yourself really feel so you can heal.

Just as mindfulness teaches us to be present in the moment, learning to recognize what your body feels is an important part of partnering with your body as you improve your health. Sometimes simply stepping back for a few moments to take some deep inhales and exhales can help you get in touch with what your body is feeling. Once you feel it, whatever the "it" is for you right now, you will then be able to name it, address it, get support for it and begin the process of healing.

Poor Health Is Expensive

I hear from many pet business owners who know they should take better care of their bodies but just don't think they can financially afford to slow down. Sometimes they are afraid of losing money or progress at a critical time in their business, while other times they have just worked through pain and illness for so long they are numb to their body's discomfort or pain or they know of no other way.

I wrote about my chiropractor friend at the beginning of this book. He waited so long to take a break from his hectic schedule that his body forced one on him in the form of a bone break. He kept telling himself he would take a break after graduation, and his body literally held him to his word. The words we speak are connected to our bodies and spirits in powerful ways. Ultimately, I see the same situation played out in one way or another for many of my coaching clients.

In the long run, you may actually *save* money by living a healthier, more conscious lifestyle. You will be sick less often, and your body will become your partner instead of something you have to cajole or force to get moving.

ESPECIALLY IN A SERVICE-BASED INDUSTRY, AND AS A SELF-EMPLOYED BUSINESS OWNER, YOU CANNOT AFFORD TO NOT TAKE CARE OF YOUR HEALTH.

Kristin's Story

A few years ago, I had a meaningful experience during my regular dental cleaning. My dentist came in after the hygienist was done and we talked about how I was grinding my teeth a bit. "It's not bad," my dentist said. "But I want you to pay attention to it." Then he asked if I was stressed. I told him that yes, I was under a bit of stress. (I was in the midst of some big work projects at the time, which often brings both excitement and some stress.)

"Are you a spiritual person?" he asked. When I told him I am, he continued, "Then you will be able to understand this. And I'm probably going to tell you something you already know, but I'm going to say it anyway: People grind their teeth because they are stressed. The mind is where stress and suffering originate. That's the only place suffering exists. In the mind. Emotions come from the mind and the thoughts you think. Do whatever you need to do to make peace with your mind. When you make peace with your mind, the stress and the grinding will stop. Personally, I meditate for 20 minutes twice a day. Whatever works for you to make peace with your mind, do it. Don't make excuses. Make having a peaceful mind your top priority."

Whoa. My perspective on stress and its physical symptoms have changed since his advice. Our teachers really do come in all shapes and forms.

Burnout Recovery Success Stories

"The price of burnout on my body is depression and a flare-up of my Lyme disease. For me, depression can be debilitating. When I have a Lyme flare-up, I experience major brain fog, bone and joint pain, muscle weakness and extreme fatigue. It takes a lot of energy just to get out of bed in the morning. I am very committed to my company and clients, so I usually power through it, but it is difficult.

I definitely go through seasons with how well I take care of myself. I can definitely be a workaholic and easily become obsessed with my work and not take the time to take care of myself. I noticed life is definitely more manageable when I do take time for myself and do the things I know work. For me, those things are checking in with my support system on a regular basis, staying in gratitude (even writing a gratitude list daily) and checking in with my feelings and motives by journaling about it. I am currently doing Morning Pages where I write a three-page letter and read it to my accountability partner. I also find taking a bath, meditating, taking a walk or hike, being in nature and enjoying a cup of tea or coffee to be beneficial.

Doing all those things on a regular, consistent basis helps me feel better and not get depressed or have a major flare-up. But also, I try to be very gentle with myself and have patience and compassion with how I show up that day or in that moment. If I don't do my self-care items like I should, I don't let myself turn it into shame."

Michelle Sabia – Paws & Claws Pet Sitting
Cave Creek, Arizona and Litchfield, Connecticut

"Stress tends to make my brain kick in as soon as I lie down and do not have the distractions of the day to keep it at bay. Thoughts whirl around and around and I either don't go to sleep for a couple of hours or wake up after two hours and can't go back to sleep. Stress also makes me more irritable, which I sometimes demonstrate to my pets or others by snapping at them.

I really have not gotten much better at self-care overall, but I have started taking time to look at aspects of my life that I believe I can work on and improve. Some of this includes reading self-help books and considering ways I can increase my knowledge on topics pertaining to my business as well as my hobbies. I am also my own worst enemy and will beat myself up over very tiny mistakes. I am learning to take deep breaths and remind myself I don't have to be perfect.

I really think it helps to step away from my life as often as I can. I have been able to do this from time to time by spending an afternoon with a friend every two or three weeks, just chatting or playing board games. If I cannot take a whole afternoon, I at least take a 30-minute walk or go sit out on the deck and read for 30 minutes from time to time. I also think it helps to find a positive goal to work towards that can help me either in my business or some personal aspect of my life. I currently provide pet sitting services, but

I've recently signed up for animal behavior classes so I can eventually help clients or shelters with difficult animals. I have also started learning clicker training to use with equines to help a horse I own and hope to apply the knowledge I gain from both the animal behavior classes and the clicker work to my business. I have also spent time looking for a way to be more involved in my community and have chosen a local nonprofit that rescues dogs from local shelters and rehabilitates them, turning them into therapy dogs. By setting such positive goals, I am hoping to reduce my burnout and improve my outlook on my life, finding more satisfaction and happiness eventually."
Barbara Link – New River Valley Pet Sitting & Farm Services, LLC
Christiansburg, Virginia

"A few years ago, I started to get shin and knee pain from all the walking I was doing. It felt sudden, like the change of seasons triggered the pain. I was 28 years old, so I was not used to seasonal stiffness quite yet. I was quite surprised when all of a sudden walking became unbearable... not great for a dog walker!

I ended up getting a good arch support for my walking shoes, which made a huge difference. The pain eventually subsided, but it forced me to slow down a bit and really think about what I needed to do to help my body cope with the strain of the job."
Stephanie Surjan – Chicago Urban Pets
Chicago, Illinois

"When it comes to what contributes to my burnout, exhaustion is number one. I need sleep or things fall apart one by one: I start forgetting things, I have no energy for anything, I get irritable and snappy and I don't handle even little things well. The lack of energy means I start not eating well because I don't have the oomph to cook anything. Some days even the microwave feels like too much. And then it's all downhill from there. I get sick easier. I have more stomach problems on a regular basis. I've even had rashes! It's an endless and unpleasant cycle that feels impossible to dig out of, which leads to a feeling of hopelessness and then to depression.

When I get to that point, I have no energy or time for things I previously enjoyed, and any downtime I do have is spent staring blankly into space because tackling anything I suddenly have time for seems like Mt. Everest. I've been there a time or two and can say that prevention literally IS the best

medicine. I have to put myself first. It is worth it. I am worth it (and so are YOU). It makes life easier and happier when I take care of myself."
Brienne Carey – BC Pet Care, LLC
Wheaton, Illinois

Action Steps – Prevent the Physical Price of Burnout

Action Step

Read through "The Physical Signs of Burnout" and make a note in your burnout recovery journal of how many symptoms on the list apply to you. Have you noticed any other physical symptoms of stress or burnout acting as warning signs to you when you need to slow down?

Action Step

Have you ever said the words, "I can't afford to take time off" or "I can't afford to be sick right now"? For many people, our bodies force us to slow down after times of intense stress with unexpected illness or aches and pains. Take some time today to reflect on how your body reacts to stress and write your thoughts in your burnout recovery journal.

Action Step

The next time you meditate or practice a mindfulness routine, take stock of how your body feels so you can FEAR—Feel Everything and Recover. Make a mental or actual list of any twinges or discomforts throughout your body.

If you haven't yet started a meditation or mindfulness habit, go back to Chapter Ten for how to get started and review the mindfulness/meditation suggestions in the *Recommended Resources* at the end of the book.

FOURTEEN

Food as Fuel

Choose What to Eat (or Not) Intentionally

"Your diet is a bank account.
Good food choices are investments."

–Bethenny Frankel

Although this chapter focuses on the food you eat, it does not contain specific dietary advice. This isn't a chapter about weight loss, macronutrients or which diet is best. Instead, I am going to encourage you to find a conscious awareness of how food works with (or against) your energy, your focus, your body and your health. As you continue to partner with your body, intentionally choosing what and when to eat will be an important key to healing and preventing burnout. When considering making any major changes in your diet, consult a doctor or a nutritionist who can evaluate your specific needs.

What Stress Does to Eating Habits

When stressed, many people eat too much, often because they are distracting themselves. Another reason stress leads to overeating is because of cortisol, one of the hormones released in times of stress, which can cause cravings for salty or sweet foods. On the other hand, some barely feel hungry at all when experiencing stress. They may lose their appetites and/or skip meals in order to get more done. In both situations, stress and burnout can lead to unhealthy relationships with food and leave your body without the nutrients it needs to function properly.

In addition to the digestive problems described in the previous chapter, stress can also have an effect on metabolism. According to the

American Psychological Association, many adults engage in unhealthy eating behaviors when stressed, leading them to feel bad about their bodies and have decreased energy.

Nutrition is important for many aspects of your life, including helping you prevent burnout. Whether you eat too much, too little or the wrong kinds of foods when you're stressed, it will be helpful for your burnout recovery to recognize how your eating habits change when you're stressed. As I mentioned at the beginning of the chapter, I am not a nutritionist, so please consult a professional if you have specific concerns about your diet.

Fueling Diets vs. Depleting Diets

Part of figuring out how to improve your nutrition is paying attention to how you feel after you eat. What foods nourish and fuel you? Which foods make you feel depleted, empty or even hungry soon after you eat? The answers to these questions will be different for each pet professional, so learning to recognize your own body's cues will be crucial.

As you learn to listen to your body's response to food and cravings, here are some general considerations to keep in mind:

1. **Redefine "comfort food."**

   Comfort food doesn't have to mean heavy, indulgent foods. Although there may be a time and a place for these, think about how you feel after you eat them: are you really more comforted or do they leave you feeling overly full and sluggish?

   Instead, pay attention to which foods really do comfort you and make you feel more energetic and nourished. Soups, smoothies and warm drinks are often very comforting and can be part of just about any dietary plan. In fact, if you search "foods to prevent burnout" online, many of the results suggest gentle, lean meals full of omega-3s and fiber — not the heavy, rich foods most people associate with "comfort."

2. **Hydrate all day long.**

   It's no secret that water is good for your body, but many people do not realize how important it actually is. According to the Harvard School of Health, drinking water does everything from helping prevent infections to improving how clearly you think to keeping your joints lubricated.

Even knowing how important hydration is, many pet professionals struggle to get enough water during the day. I recommend always preparing at least one large water bottle for the day — there are a number of vacuum-sealed containers available now that will keep your water ice cold all day without dripping — and refilling it often. According to Mayo Clinic, most men need around 15.5 cups of fluid in a day, while women should get around 11.5 cups. These recommendations include any beverages or fluid from foods, but they are only guidelines. Your individual needs may be different, especially if you live in a particularly warm or humid area or have other health conditions that affect your hydration.

> **Burnout Recovery Tip**
> If you aren't drinking enough water, use the same tricks you've found work for your other goals: set yourself a reminder, track your progress on an app, find an accountability buddy or treat yourself to a reward after reaching milestones.

3. **Establish a better relationship with caffeine.**
   Depending on how you feel after drinking coffee, soda or tea, you may need to scale back your caffeine intake... or at least be more intentional about how much you consume and when.

   The main issue with caffeine is the way it affects your mood. Caffeine intake can prompt the release of hormones into your blood. This is one of the ways caffeine helps you stay awake, but it can also lead to uncomfortable side effects for some. Some people can sleep soundly after a large cup of coffee, while others can't have any caffeine in the afternoon and still fall asleep on time. For some, caffeine is a mood booster. For others, it increases anxiety and stress. If you aren't sure how caffeine is affecting you, consider going without it for a few days and then slowly reintroducing it into your diet, paying attention to how it makes you feel as you do.

When You Eat Matters, Too

When you eat can matter as much as *what* you eat. If you go too long without a snack or a meal, you may find your attention waning or feel annoyed more easily. If you eat too late in the day, you may have difficulty sleeping or feel uncomfortable as your body tries to digest a big meal at night.

IN MANY CASES, **WHEN** YOU EAT CAN MATTER AS MUCH AS **WHAT** YOU EAT.

For many pet professionals, finding time to eat during the day (let alone to prepare a nutritious meal) is a real challenge. In fact, I have a number of coaching clients who want to make sure they find time to eat healthy food. Does this sound familiar? How often have you skipped a meal because you didn't have time to eat? How often have you eaten quickly in your car between clients? And how do you feel on days like this? Pre-planning and scheduling smaller, more regular meals have been the keys to many business owners feeling better throughout the day — giving them the energy and health they need to do their job and help prevent burnout.

As you evaluate the timing of your own meals, here are three tips to making your own nutrition a priority:

1. **Schedule specific time(s) to eat.**
   In the time plan example I share in Chapter Seven, my client realized she needed to prioritize smaller meals throughout the day. As a result of that awareness, she blocked out more time for meals in her ideal time plan as a way to hold herself accountable and give herself permission to stop and eat. If you struggle to fit mealtime into your busy day, or if you find yourself eating too much at night, you may need to make snacks and meals part of your daily schedule.

2. **Plan your meals in advance.**
   It is all too easy to make poor choices when you are tired, overwhelmed or in a hurry. Whether you want to eat less, eat more nutritious foods or eat a more complete meal, planning your meals in advance can be a major help. Rather than grabbing whatever is closest or sounds best at the time (a recipe for poor choices if you are already exhausted and

burned out by the time you eat), decide ahead of time what meals and snacks to eat in a day or week. Many pet business owners find it helpful to keep healthy snacks in their car or in their office. The same idea is true for meals — planning out your meals, even if it's just one or two days in advance, can help you make more intentional choices.

3. **Budget time and money for meal prep.**
   Nutritious, fueling meals do not have to be overly complicated or expensive, but they may take more time, and even a bit more money, than simply grabbing whatever is at hand. Don't let this keep you from making better food choices; your health is worth it!

As with most aspects of burnout recovery and prevention, your personal preferences should influence your approach. If you find cooking enjoyable, give yourself more time and money for ingredients and trying new recipes. If you do not enjoy cooking, you may consider a meal service, either the kind that sends you recipes and ingredients or deliveries of completed meals — or having someone come and prepare meals for you. There are more solutions than ever for busy professionals looking for help with nutrition. You can find some in the *Recommended Resources* section.

In this chapter's *Action Steps*, I will encourage you to figure out what you need to improve your nutrition and the timing of your meals. As you make a schedule, plan time for your meals into your daily schedule and budget food prep time and money for better health — all of which get easier with practice. After a period of time of healthful eating, you will likely see an increase in energy and health. Over time, it will get easier to prioritize your health.

Kristin's Story

In the past year I've made two big changes when it comes to food, and both have helped me be healthier and happier. The first positive change was signing up for a meal-prep delivery service. At the end of a workday, one of the last tasks my husband and I want to do is cook — and eating out or restaurant delivery can be quite expensive over time and result in eating higher calorie foods than we would if we were preparing food in our home. We decided to sign up for a healthy meal-prep delivery service, so now, every Wednesday afternoon we get a box delivered with ingredients for three healthy dinners for two each week. This has taken the guesswork out of cooking for at least three nights a week! Although we still have to cook, everything is planned out and all ingredients are included, so all we have to do is chop, follow the recipe, and in less than 30 minutes, we've got a healthy dinner. It's been a game changer for us!

The second big change I've made is tracking everything I eat. Just like tracking each purchase has been helpful personally and professionally, tracking my calories has created a mindfulness within me about exactly what and how much I'm eating and drinking. This information has helped me make profound changes in what and how much I'm consuming. Because of daily tracking, I've easily lost some weight and feel great!

Burnout Recovery Success Stories

"I have learned I have to eat, and on a regular schedule. On quieter days, I can get away with the standard three meals, but on a busy day, I need to eat smaller meals more frequently. On those days, I eat about five times spaced out throughout the day. These smaller meals keep my energy and blood pressure more stable. Otherwise, it will bottom out and I'll feel sick and shaky, and I'll feel like I'm about to pass out.

I don't always worry about what I'm eating; what's important for me is that I do eat. Mostly, I try to eat as balanced of a meal as possible, but I'll be the first to admit the whole fruit/veggie thing can be quite the task! I keep stashes of granola bars and trail mixes on hand for emergency backup."
Brienne Carey – BC Pet Care, LLC
Wheaton, Illinois

"I struggle with low blood sugar at times, so when I go a certain amount of time without eating, I start feeling really nauseous, even if I might not necessarily be hungry. I've learned this the hard way when running out early in the morning and then being stuck at a bus stop with nothing to eat and feeling like I'm going to faint.

When I was personally in the field full time, I would try and have snacks in my bag at all times for those exact instances because I'd end up regretting it later if I left without them. Since many dog walks are during lunch time (11-2), I'd usually have something filling to eat before I left the house and then eat again when I returned home.

Being so active with my job (we are in the city and don't drive between homes, instead we walk or take public transit), I was less sensitive to what I ate because I was burning it so fast. (I was also in my 20s.) But I definitely think it's important to fit in fruit and veggies throughout the day to maintain a healthy and well-rounded diet.

I think in the long run, I am able to sustain hard times better if I am already living a balanced life, which includes what I eat."
Stephanie Surjan – Chicago Urban Pets
Chicago, Illinois

"Food is super important and ties right along with taking care of myself, mind, body and soul. If I am on the verge of burnout, it probably means I'm not feeding myself well. I typically will go all day without eating almost anything and then binge on a very large meal for dinner. I definitely feel a positive difference when I snack throughout the day and try to get in good nutritious foods and lots of water! I do my best to always drink a gallon of water a day. For me, not having any alcohol is also super important!"
Michelle Sabia – Paws & Claws Pet Sitting
Cave Creek, Arizona and Litchfield, Connecticut

"I completely switched my way of eating. Previously, I would snack on nothing but junk food and ate meat-based meals. After discovering the book Superlife, I am now switching over to a mostly plant-based diet. I am not going vegan, but I have committed to reducing my dairy intake (there's actually nondairy cheese and ice cream products that are delicious) and eating several small 'meals' a day mostly made up of raw food such as salads and fruit. Eating meat always tended to make me feel tired and bloated or uncomfortably full. Eating plants still fills me up, but I am now not uncomfortable after a meal. I have more energy, and even more importantly, I feel like I am making an environmentally sound choice as well, which improves my mood, satisfaction and esteem."
Barbara Link – New River Valley Pet Sitting & Farm Services, LLC
Christiansburg, Virginia

Action Steps – Food as Fuel

Action Step

How does your relationship with food change when you are stressed? Before you can make any decisions about dietary changes, it helps to be aware of your current patterns. Read through the earlier section "What Stress Does to Eating Habits" and identify if you are a stress eater, a meal skipper or somewhere in between. Making this distinction will help you make a healthier food plan in the following *Action Steps* because you will know your starting point before making any changes.

Action Step

For the next week, track everything you eat and drink. At the end of each meal (or each day if each meal feels too restrictive), make a note of how you feel. How much water have you been drinking on an average day? Which foods or habits are more fueling? Which are more depleting? Have you noticed any other physical effects (either positive or negative) you can attribute to what you eat/drink?

Action Step

Using the notes you made while tracking your meals, make a list in your burnout recovery journal of fueling foods/habits you want to encourage and depleting foods/habits you plan to avoid. Then, identify what you need to do or change to make these fueling foods/habits part of your regular routine. Check the *Recommended Resources* section for suggestions you may find useful as you make your list of improvements.

Action Step

Choose at least two new nutrition habits or routines to cultivate for the next month. These habits might be eating more regularly, prepping meals in advance or drinking more water. Use the productivity and goal-setting patterns you established in Chapter Seven and the resources in the *Recommended Resources* section to hold yourself accountable for these new habits for the month.

At the end of the month, write in your burnout recovery journal about the experience. What has gotten better and what do you still want to improve? What differences have you noticed in your health and energy? Has it gotten easier to achieve your nutrition goals?

FIFTEEN

Savor Sleep

Maximize the Restorative Power of Sleep

*"Sleep is the golden chain that binds health and
our bodies together."*

–Thomas Dekker

The importance of sleep is probably something you have already thought about if you're feeling burned out. Because sleep deprivation is common in such a large percentage of people, many studies have been done about the benefits of sleep and the risks of not getting enough. Using some of that research and the personal experiences of other pet business owners, this chapter will focus on what sleep can do for your burnout recovery and how you can get better sleep, even if you have a full work schedule. Rather than taking time away from your work and limiting what you can do in a day, like many people assume it will, more sleep will actually make you more productive because of the mood and energy boost better sleep brings. Many of my coaching clients describe their burnout with words like "tired," "exhausted" or "drained." If you feel that way now or in the future, maximizing the restorative power of sleep may be even more helpful than you realize.

The Role of Sleep in Burnout Prevention or Recovery

Sleep is incredibly important for both day-to-day quality of life and your long-term health. More than that, a good night's sleep can help you in your role as business owner as well because sleep affects your mood and your ability to make decisions.

According to the Harvard Medical School, even partial sleep deprivation can have a negative impact on your mood. On the other hand, after even a single week of better sleep, most study participants reported dramatic improvements in their moods. Your job as a pet professional requires you to be alert, and if you work closely with clients, to be approachable and friendly. Think about how you feel and react after a rough night of little sleep. Are you calm and patient with your staff members and clients, or are you short-tempered? If for no other reason, sleep should be a priority because of how you interact with others after a good night's sleep.

In addition to mood, sleep matters when you make decisions as well. You may have already noticed this connection in your own life. Is it easier to make clear, forward-thinking decisions when you have enough sleep? For many people, the answer is "yes." Making conscious, intentional decisions for your business and for your personal life — the kinds of decisions that will have long-lasting impact and help you find balance and joy — is easier to do when you are sleeping well. Chronic stress and anxiety often make it difficult for people to sleep. There may be nights or even weeks when it is harder to sleep than you'd like. But that doesn't mean you should give up and discard the idea of achieving regular, restorative sleep. After all the work you've put in, both reflecting on your current situation as you read this book and completing the *Action Steps* in order to better understand and address the underlying causes of your burnout, don't disregard this chapter because of your past experiences with sleep. Allow better rest to be an additional help in preventing future burnout by prioritizing sleep.

> IF FOR NO OTHER REASON, SLEEP SHOULD BE A PRIORITY BECAUSE OF HOW YOU INTERACT WITH OTHERS ON A GOOD NIGHT'S SLEEP.

Getting Enough Sleep

Do you know how much sleep you are getting most nights? As with most aspects of burnout recovery and prevention, figuring out where you are now is the first step to improvement. Once you know how much sleep you are actually getting, you will have a better idea of whether you need more sleep every night, more consistent sleep or simply to improve the quality of your sleep. In this chapter's *Action*

Steps, I will give you an assignment to track your sleep for two weeks. I've also included some suggested apps to help you manage and track your sleep in the *Recommended Resources* section at the end of this book.

As for how much sleep you need, the answer does vary from person to person. Even with personal variation, the CDC, Mayo Clinic and the National Sleep Foundation all agree that people over the age of 18 should get between seven and nine hours of sleep per night. Your activity level, health and personal medical history may also affect the amount of sleep your body needs every night.

These questions from the National Sleep Foundation are designed to help you determine if you need the minimum seven hours of sleep or if you might benefit from closer to nine hours each night:

- Are you productive, healthy, and happy on seven hours of sleep? Or have you noticed that you require more hours of sleep to get into high gear?

- Do you have coexisting health issues? Are you at higher risk for any disease?

- Do you have a high level of daily energy expenditure? Do you frequently play sports, exercise or work in a labor-intensive job?

- Do your daily activities require alertness to do them safely? Do you drive every day and/or operate heavy machinery? Do you ever feel sleepy when doing these activities?

- Are you experiencing, or do you have a history of, sleeping problems?

- Do you depend on caffeine to get you through the day?

- When you have an open schedule, do you sleep more than you do on a typical workday?

In addition to your answers to these questions, keep in mind the seven-to nine-hour recommendation is for total hours of sleep, not necessarily continuous hours of sleep. It is normal for older adults to start sleeping less at one time than they did when they were younger. They are often lighter sleepers and get their hours over a few separate sleep sessions.

Many pet professionals are overworked and exhausted much of the time, so I've given you many tools you can use to deal with your stress and lighten your load throughout this book. No matter where you are in your efforts to make those changes, getting enough quality sleep is an important aspect of burnout recovery. If you didn't know it already, tracking your sleep and reading this chapter may help you realize you need more sleep. If that's the case, your next question may be *how* and *when* to fit in more sleep.

Here are five tested and proven suggestions from my own experience and the experiences of other business owners and entrepreneurs:

1. **Put sleep in your schedule.**

   Just as I've had clients schedule time for meals as they try to improve what they eat, start scheduling your sleep. In addition to scheduling a time to go to bed at night, consider scheduling in occasional or regular afternoon naps (more on those later). Even if you don't fall asleep right away, scheduling time for sleep may help keep you accountable to yourself.

2. **Make sleep a priority.**

   As the saying goes, *if it matters, you will make time.* You may intend to add sleep to your schedule, as recommended in the previous suggestion, but if sleep is not a priority, you may find yourself using that scheduled sleep time for other activities. Unfortunately, even though we know sleep is good for us, it is often one of the first things we cut out or shorten when faced with too much to do and not enough time.

   > **Burnout Recovery Tip**
   > If you are struggling to find time to get enough sleep, you may need to start with understanding its importance. Research sleep studies, journal how you feel and act when you are tired versus rested or use another approach that helps you understand the importance of sleep.

3. **Set an alarm — for going to bed.**

   Once you've scheduled your bedtime, stick to it. That might mean setting an alarm of one kind or another. If you have the option to turn off your internet at a certain time each night or lights you can program by time of day, scheduling an evening shutdown/turn off can help you get to bed.

4. **Try napping.**

   As I wrote earlier in this section, most sleep experts consider any sleep during a 24-hour period as counting toward your daily total. While long naps may leave you feeling groggy and keep you from sleeping at night, a short power nap in the middle of the day might be what you need to increase your sleeping hours and give you the energy you need to finish the day. I had a client once who would take a *siesta* after the afternoon dog walks each day and found herself revitalized and refreshed before she attended to returning client emails and calls before her workday was complete.

5. **Let staff members handle the early or late shift hours.**

   I regularly hear from pet business owners how transitioning their early and late appointments/duties to staff members revolutionizes their mornings or evenings. Sleeping in a bit later in the day is one benefit of having someone else take the morning shift, while having a staff member handle the evening work hours may help you more easily stick to a regular evening bedtime. Even if you don't—or can't—sleep later, you will have more time for your morning routine and to prepare for the day before you have to hit the ground running.

I completely understand that it is not always easy to get enough sleep, but the benefits are worth whatever effort it takes to get to a place of regularly getting enough sleep because prioritizing sleep can help you recover from burnout. However, it's not enough to just sleep *more*. You also need to sleep *well* if you want to make the most of the healing power of sleep.

How to Improve the Quality of Your Sleep

It is common for sleep quality to decline during times of high stress. If you are experiencing burnout, you may toss and turn, struggle to fall or stay asleep or continue to feel sluggish and drained, even after what seems like a full night's sleep when you've looked at how many hours you've slept.

As you partner with your body to restore yourself and heal from burnout (and continue to prevent burnout moving forward), here are seven ways to improve the quality of your sleep:

1. **Be consistent with sleep and wake times.**

   When it comes to energy levels and focus, consistency of sleep matters more than the number of hours you get. When you go to sleep and wake up at approximately the same time every day, your body gets used to the pattern. You will likely start to feel drowsy at the same time and have an easier time waking up in the morning, even without an alarm.

2. **Establish a bedtime routine.**

   In addition to setting a time to go to bed each night, design a bedtime routine that helps you relax and mentally prepare for bed. This routine might include a shower or bath, meditation, journaling, listening to music or doing some light reading. Many of the topics previously covered in this book can be used as suggestions and starting points for your bedtime routine. Go back to Chapter Ten for more detailed information about meditation or to Chapter Nine for guidance on the best kind of nurturing activities for you. After a week or more of sticking to this bedtime routine, you will likely discover your body and mind preparing for sleep as you go through the steps of your routine.

3. **Avoid the blue light of screens before bed.**

   Phones, computers, televisions and many energy-efficient lights emit what is called "blue light" because of its blue wavelengths. This type of light may boost productivity and focus, but both focus and productivity can make it challenging to fall (and stay) asleep. Exposure to any kind of light at night can interrupt the body's natural rhythms and contribute to trouble sleeping, but blue light especially so. Reducing exposure to blue lights two to three hours before bed will probably improve the quality of your sleep.

   Another benefit to disconnecting digitally a few hours before bed is that you will be able to mentally separate your thoughts from the constant demands of email, social media, etc. It will also be a built-in buffer when you can turn off your "business owner" side and just be *you*. I have heard from many clients who initially wondered what they would ever find to do in the hours before bed without their phone. Before long, many of them reported looking forward to those hours most in every day as a time to pursue a hobby, connect with family or relax.

4. **Create a restful environment.**
When it is time to go to sleep, do you fall asleep quickly? While you cannot change all of the reasons you may or may not go to sleep easily, there are quite a few you can control. Create a restful environment in your bedroom so you have a retreat from the stress of your day. While the ideal bedroom setup will be a little bit different reader to reader, some ideas include using essential oils or other gentle fragrance designed to promote relaxation, blocking out light with blackout curtains, investing in a white noise machine or app if you like white noise, or removing any sources of noise if you prefer silence. You may consider not charging your phone right next to the bed, for example, if it emits lights and noises that disturb you throughout the night. Another option is to turn on your phone's version of Do Not Disturb or Night mode, so you do not get notifications during your sleeping hours but can still keep your phone nearby for emergencies or to take advantage of sleep or alarm apps.

5. **Work with your body's internal clock, not against it.**
Entire books have been written about your body's circadian rhythm (and you can find some in the *Reading List* if this topic is of special interest to you). At its most basic, "circadian rhythm" is a term to describe the natural cycle of alertness and drowsiness all bodies experience every day. Ideally, you will work with your body's natural rhythms to wake up and fall asleep more easily rather than struggling against them.

For example, every hour you sleep before midnight affects your circadian rhythm in a powerful, positive way. There is research to suggest the first full sleep cycle is the most restorative and deeper because non-REM sleep (which includes three cycles of its own) is responsible for how rested you feel when you wake up, though both REM and non-REM sleep has benefits. Some researchers believe the amount of non-REM sleep you get depends on the time of night you sleep and not just the number of hours.

If you are naturally a night owl, you can still maximize your restorative sleep by setting a reasonable bedtime — even if that bedtime is later than some. You can also gradually change your body's internal clock. I know, because I did it. In this chapter's *Kristin's Story*, I share my own sleep experience, including how I changed from being a night owl to a morning person.

6. **Meditate.**

The benefits of meditation have already been described in detail in Chapter Ten. However, when it comes to falling and staying asleep, meditation has another potential benefit — clearing your mind and focusing on the moment can help you calm down and relax before bed. Meditation slows your heart rate and breathing naturally, preparing you for sleep. In fact, there are entire guided meditations designed to be done before bed or even in bed as you fall asleep. I've included a link to one such guided meditation in the *Recommended Resources*, or you can search online for "meditation for falling asleep" for more options.

7. **Adjust your afternoon.**

Napping and consuming caffeine late in the day have been shown to prevent sleep in some people. This leads to a vicious cycle of napping or drinking coffee to stay awake because you didn't sleep well, only to not be able to sleep again the next night. There is no hard and fast rule about how late is too late for that last cup of coffee or power nap, so you will want to figure out for yourself what time in the afternoon to start limiting activities that keep you from falling asleep at night.

For some people, working out in the evening makes it harder to fall asleep. If this is true for you, you'll want to plan exercise time earlier in the day. Drinking too much water before bed can also be problematic if you are up and down all night going to the restroom. As you design and modify your own bedtime routine and schedule, keep track of what activities seem to encourage sleep and which should be kept to the beginning of the day.

As with many of the suggestions in this book, these tips for getting better sleep will be most helpful when you discover what works for *you* — enabling you to get the most out of your sleep and truly rest.

Kristin's Story

I used to be a night owl and assumed that's what I would always be... and then I met my husband. Our partner's sleep schedule can affect us, and my partner wakes up very (very) early. Even if I wake up what feels like very early for me, I can almost always bet he's already awake. For some time after we met, I tried continuing my night owl routine, but it just wasn't possible to be both a night owl and wake up so early with him. Going to bed late and waking up early is not sustainable — at least not for me. I realized something had to give.

Even knowing something needed to change, I was reluctant to let go of being a "night owl" — I very much identified it as a part of who I was. I soon realized if I wanted to both be in this relationship (which I did) and get quality sleep (which I needed), I would need to take care of myself by going to bed earlier. I now get tired and go to bed at around 10pm instead of my previous midnight or 1am bedtime.

My husband sometimes snores and because of that, I will sometimes sleep in our spare room. We both had a lot of feelings come up around my sleeping in another room, but the bottom line again is that if my sleep suffers, I suffer. And I'm opposed to suffering! When I'm lacking in sleep (both quality and quantity), my husband reaps the negative impact of that too, as I'm often crabby, irritable and moody. So even though it has been an adjustment, he has come to appreciate the benefits of me occasionally sleeping in the guest room in order to get enough rest.

I really have made it a point to prioritize sleep because when I don't, it affects me and my life in a negative and profound way. I am unwilling to accept those negative effects, so getting adequate sleep — which for me means eight to nine hours a night — is non-negotiable because of the impact sleep has on my body, mind and spirit. It's a positive impact when I get my daily sleep quota and a negative impact when I don't get my body's preferred sleep quota. Sleep truly is at the very top of my self-care list and I've learned to make it a priority.

Burnout Recovery Success Stories

"I do my best to get at least eight hours of sleep a night. I typically sleep pretty well through the night, though I do toss and turn a lot. I try not to be on my phone right before I fall asleep. That definitely helps the quality of sleep I get. Having a routine right before bed and right when I wake up in the morning helps to get a restful night's sleep and a more productive day. I don't nap often but know how great a good nap can feel. Even meditating for 15 minutes can feel like I got in a good power nap."
Michelle Sabia – Paws & Claws Pet Sitting
Cave Creek, Arizona and Litchfield, Connecticut

"I am very lucky if I get a good night's sleep. I don't do naps very often. Brief naps, when I do take one, perk me up for a short period of time during the day. What helps me most is to go to bed at the same time each night, early enough to read in bed for about half an hour. I like to pick a fun, relaxing book that I can get lost in to help calm my mind and make me sleepy. I also keep a couple of all-natural remedies on hand, one is a sleep aid and one is for calming the mind. If I am having issues, I take one or the other. This generally helps, but as of yet, I do not get a great night of sleep very often. What has helped the most is having my employee take all morning visits so I don't have to get up as early, so I can have an extended 'wake up' period in the mornings."
Barbara Link – New River Valley Pet Sitting & Farm Services, LLC
Christiansburg, Virginia

"I slept well when I was dog walking and was so physically active during the day! I regularly got my solid nine hours in, which feels super luxurious now that I have a toddler in the home and haven't had a good night's sleep in two years!

In general, when talking about a balanced life, there are all these pieces of a puzzle that need to be in their place in order for the image to appear. Diet and sleep are both parts of that puzzle. My sleep piece is currently not in its place right now, which has an effect on other aspects of my life. It affects my mood because when I'm tired, I'm more short-tempered and less flexible. It affects my diet because I'm too tired to cook balanced meals and end up eating crackers and cheese or anything which is a quick fix. It affects my productivity because I'm always trying to recoup that lost energy instead of focusing on what needs to be done.

Something that has helped a lot with sleep has been breastfeeding and sharing my bed with my baby, who is now a toddler. The fact that I had to lay in bed with him every time he slept due to breastfeeding allowed me time to rest and possibly sleep too. Taking that time during the day to snuggle in with my baby and nap has helped me keep my sanity as a mother and business owner."
Stephanie Surjan – Chicago Urban Pets
Chicago, Illinois

"Sleep is the number one most important thing that I need. It's been that way my entire life; I am just one of those people that needs a lot of sleep. That's been the best thing about working for myself – I start and end my day as I wish, so I can be sure I get the sleep that I need, and I do not budge on that. Most nights, I sleep pretty well, for the most part. I do have streaks where I struggle a few nights here and there. There's a pillow spray called 'This Works' that I do actually think works for helping me sleep. I also need it to be pitch black and either silent or with white noise. No in-between. Gentle stretching before bed is helpful too and maybe a little reading. I shower at night too as the hot water is relaxing and clarifying.

I also nap when I need it, about a half-hour max. Any longer and it makes me groggy, as opposed to feeling more refreshed. I'm a fan of 'caffeine naps' although I don't do those as often as when I was younger as I drink less caffeine. Basically, I drink a cup of coffee and then take a power nap. By the time I'm waking up from my nap, the caffeine is kicking in and I'm ready to get moving."
Brienne Carey – BC Pet Care, LLC
Wheaton, Illinois

Action Steps – Savor Sleep

Action Step

For the next two weeks, record when you fall asleep and wake up each day. If you take naps, make note of how long they last as well. This information will give you a starting point for any changes you need to make to your sleep schedule. Check the *Recommended Resources* section for some apps and tools for tracking your sleep cycles automatically if you prefer.

Action Step

Go through the National Sleep Foundation questions listed in the "Getting Enough Sleep" section of this chapter and answer them in your burnout recovery journal. Looking through your answers, do you think you need closer to seven or nine hours of sleep? How does this compare to what you are currently getting?

Action Step

Choose at least two suggestions in the "Getting Enough Sleep" section and commit to making any necessary changes in your personal life or business. If you choose to let staff members handle the early appointments, for example, you may need to hire more staff or get the ones you have accustomed to the early morning duties.

Action Step

Design a bedtime routine that will help you unwind and relax before bed. Use the suggestions in the chapter or do an internet search for "what to do before bed" for a variety of articles and suggestions on recommended bedtime routines. Once you have written down your ideal routine, stick to it for at least a week. After the week, write in your burnout recovery journal any changes you notice in yourself or in your sleep thanks to your new bedtime routine.

Exercise More Effectively

Regular Body Movement for Burnout Prevention and Recovery

"When it comes to health and well-being, regular exercise is about as close to a magic potion as you can get."

–Thich Nhat Hanh

The final chapter in this section about partnering with your body in your burnout recovery focuses on exercise. "But Kristin," you might be saying, "how does adding one more item to my list of *should-dos* help me feel less burned out?" If seeing a chapter on exercise immediately fills you with guilt or feelings of not measuring up, take heart. This chapter is about how moving your body will help your mood, your business and your health... not about maximizing your physical gains or reaching any particular level of fitness. You will not find workout advice or routines here; instead, you will read reasons to include regular activity in your schedule and how it can help you recover from, and prevent, burnout.

The Physical, Mental and Emotional Benefits of Exercise

It is well understood by researchers and medical professionals at this point that regular exercise is good for you. The main benefits of exercise can be divided into three categories—physical, mental and emotional. While I won't dwell on *why* you should exercise, I will quickly summarize some of the many positive effects exercise can have for you.

The Physical Benefits

Regular physical activity, especially the kind that elevates your heart rate for at least 30 minutes, is good for your heart health. Blood sugar, weight and high blood pressure can all be managed in part by exercise. Exercising regularly has also been shown to help patients quit smoking, manage chronic arthritis and improve bone density.

The Mental Benefits

In addition to making your body stronger, exercise is also good for your mind. Exercise has been shown to reduce anxiety, help with mild depression and release chemicals in your body that make stress easier to manage. If you are trying to prevent burnout from business-related stress, any reduction in stress and anxiety is a positive. I will also write more about the mental and creativity boost that physical activity gives me (and many others) later in the chapter.

The Emotional Benefits

Like I mentioned in the chapter on sleep, being in a balanced place emotionally is especially important for pet professionals because of the caregiving and client interactions involved in your job. Exercise can stabilize your mood and help you approach problems without pent-up emotion or frustration. Exercising with friends or family is also a fun way to strengthen those relationships and build emotional connections.

> EXERCISE HAS BEEN SHOWN TO REDUCE ANXIETY, HELP WITH MILD DEPRESSION AND RELEASE CHEMICALS IN YOUR BODY THAT MAKE STRESS EASIER TO MANAGE.

For many busy business owners, it can be difficult to fit regular exercise into each day. Understanding the variety and magnitude of improvements physical activity can bring about in your life makes it too important to pass up, especially when you see how it can help you build your business as well.

Regular Movement Encourages Creativity

One of the first changes I made when my pet care business grew to the point where I stopped doing dog walks myself was to institute an hour-long hike each day. This is a ritual I have continued for many years because of the incredible benefits I've found, including the mind-body connection I find while exercising.

I initially began this daily hike as a way to stay active, but it has become so much more. After I write my Morning Pages and check voicemail and emails, I head out for a morning hike. What I discovered pretty early on was my mind would wander during the hike, leading me to some of my best ideas and strategies. I regularly come home from my hikes with realizations about conversations I need to have with a staff member or steps I need to take personally. The combination of Morning Pages and physical activity has been so powerful for me because it kicks my brain into creative mode and enables me to be focused and intentional the rest of the day.

I have also noticed that when I change trails, I don't notice the same mental focus right away. I think this is because hiking the same trail over and over allows my mind to wander because I do not need to think about where to go. I know the trail like the back of my hand, which frees up my mental space for creativity and ideas. It's similar to how so many people have great ideas in the shower — physical repetition and mental wandering can lead to some powerful discoveries.

For you, this spark may not come on a hike. You may find it swimming laps, doing yoga or during Tai Chi. Any movement you can do while letting your mind wander is ideal for a daily exercise to open your mind to clarity.

Tips for Fitting Exercise into a Busy Schedule

Even knowing how important physical activity can be, I still hear from clients who just don't think they have time for regular exercise. I hope, by the time you get to this chapter, you will have better strategies for making time in your schedule for priorities than you did before you picked up the book. Still, it can be helpful to hear what works for other pet professionals, which is why I've included their success stories at the end of the chapter.

I've also compiled the top five strategies I've found for fitting exercise into a busy schedule — in my own life and the work I do with coaching clients:

1. **Figure out what type of exercise works best for you.**

   I already wrote about how my daily hike is perfect for me, but your needs will be different than mine. If your work requires you to be physically active, you may want a lower-impact activity like yoga. Some people prefer to work out in the morning, while others find it best to finish the day at the gym. Figure out what activities and times of day are best for you so you can make a plan for *you*.

2. **Schedule time to exercise.**

   If you don't block time out of your time plan for exercise, it will probably not happen. You will probably always have another task to do or someone demanding your attention. Carve time out of each week's schedule for dedicated exercise and stick to it.

3. **If you get stuck, mix up your workouts.**

   The same workout routine may be perfect for years and then suddenly... not. Trying something new may be a good way to reenergize your exercise. Take some classes, join a sports league or take an evening walk. You might also consider adding in weight training. Even small amounts of weight resistance can help build strength and give you a new goal to work toward.

4. **Work out with someone else.**

   Invite a friend or family member to be part of your exercise routine. Not only will you have someone to keep you accountable, you will be able to strengthen your relationship and have someone to talk to at the same time. As much as I encourage this strategy, please note that working out with someone else will keep you from the mind-wandering freedom of a repetitive, solo exercise. If you plan to work out with someone else, consider adding daily solo movement for the creative space it may give your mind.

5. **Have a backup plan.**

   Even the most avid athletes occasionally have their training plans interrupted. Having a plan for when things go wrong will help you stay on track. For example, what will you do when it rains or snows (if you exercise outside)? What kind of workout can you use on days you have a minor injury? I suggest a backup exercise you can do at home for days when your ideal plan falls through.

In this chapter's *Action Steps*, I will encourage you to figure out which of these suggestions you can use to make the most of physical movement and to set a goal for yourself. Setting a goal — for more regular exercise, for a certain physical milestone or simply to try something new — can energize your workout routine and help you strengthen your body at the same time. You only have one body — you might as well take care of it!

> **Burnout Recovery Tip**
> For many people, having a daily movement goal can help increase their exercise for the day. Many apps and some watches will count your steps for you. Check the **Recommended Resources** section for ideas if you know you'll benefit from the external encouragement of reminders to meet your daily activity goal.

Kristin's Story

During the COVID-19 pandemic, my regular workout routine got profoundly interrupted. I previously had a regular gym routine four to five times a week, and I was suddenly unable to go to the gym at all. For a few months, I felt unmoored when it came to exercise and I essentially stopped exercising — I had become used to my routine and then it was suddenly not an option. I no longer lived right next door to my beloved hiking trail (the trail I write about in this chapter) and I depended on the gym for regular exercise. Like getting sleep, not exercising is not sustainable for me. Having a period of time where I was not exercising regularly made that very apparent! The lack of exercise affected my body, mind and spirit in negative ways, and after a while, I knew I needed to exercise more than ever during the pandemic — instead of exercising less or not at all.

When it comes to exercise, at least for me, convenience is crucial. If my exercise destination takes a while to get to, or the exercise is too complicated, I often won't do it. I know this about myself, so I realized

I had to find an alternate solution now that my gym was closed, and my beloved hiking trail was now a few miles away from my home. I found a trail that I could walk to from my new home and began walking that trail a few times a week. It's not my ideal trail—I tend to prefer private, peaceful trails in the woods and this one is a well-populated path on a marsh without many trees around (which is why I'd avoided it until I got desperate for exercise!)—but it's close, and that helps me actually do it. When I'm having a hard time getting myself out the door to go on my "marsh walk," I will entice myself to go by taking my phone and headphones and chatting with a friend or listening to a podcast episode I've been wanting to hear, though I usually leave my phone at home so I can connect with myself, the marshy nature that surrounds me and my thoughts, goals and dreams.

Burnout Recovery Success Stories

"When I am feeling burnout in this field of work, I don't think that getting more physical exercise is the solution. That may be just me. However, if you are the type that enjoys problem solving while taking a jog, you should definitely continue that. Personally, it was important for me to set boundaries because usually burnout is about overextension.

I love the analogy of the jar with the big and small rocks. The way it goes is that the big rocks are your priorities and the small rocks are all the other tasks that need to be done. If you put your big rocks in first, the small rocks will fill the jar around the big rocks. But if you fill the jar with all the small rocks first, your big rocks won't fit anymore. That to me is burnout."
Stephanie Surjan – Chicago Urban Pets
Chicago, Illinois

"As a dog walker, I definitely try to make it a point to take a walk just by myself without a dog. It's also a good way for me to connect to nature and meditate. I just feel more peaceful and connected after a walk or hike in nature. My aunt is an artist here in Arizona, and I'll never forget her telling me that hiking was so important for her because that's where she got all of her ideas for her art. I feel the same way about being a business owner. It's like when I am out there hiking, I feel so connected and inspired and

clearheaded! Usually after I have a good hike, I'm craving really nutritious yummy foods! And then I usually have a really good day following that. Also, getting regular movement, my body typically feels better and has less joint pain. It also helps with my depression."
Michelle Sabia – Paws & Claws Pet Sitting
Cave Creek, Arizona and Litchfield, Connecticut

"Exercise is good... when I have energy for it! Sometimes exercise helps increase my energy and other times it's just a bad idea and I need a nap instead. I've learned to listen to my body. Stretching is my favorite thing, whether it's yoga or just simple stretching routines. It always feels so good! Walking is also pretty easy to get in when you're a dog walker. I also enjoy dance routines or barre or some HIIT routines, etc. I can't stick to just one thing or I get bored. Variety is key or I won't do it. I love having an active job because it keeps me fit without having to think about it. Work smarter, not harder!

One of the best things I've learned is to give myself five minutes... everyone has five minutes. I can't say there's no time for exercise when even five minutes makes a difference. It's great on days where I feel like I don't have the time. It's a start! It's better than standing still and continuing to do zilch. Five minutes = change your life. That applies to so many things, including exercise.

Bodies were made to move, so it's important to move them. It keeps a number of health issues away and helps with stress and just puts me in a better mood. I think it's highly important to keep in shape to keep up with the doggos, too. There's less possibility for injury that way!"
Brienne Carey – BC Pet Care, LLC
Wheaton, Illinois

"Until very recently, I was not able to have exercise as part of my routine due to a knee issue and a Morton's neuroma. Now that the neuroma is better, I am in PT for the knee, and am doing daily exercises every morning and walking again. I am also starting to hike and to work my horses. Spending time with my horses and hiking on beautiful trails in the mountains of Virginia always relaxes me and does wonders for my mood. I

make it a point to do any exercises first thing in the morning after feeding the pets, so the day does not get in the way of getting them done. This helps me to focus and keep on track. It also helps to wake me up and energize me. I have a full-time job besides my pet business, so I make a point to get up about every half hour and move throughout the day as well, to keep my mind and body alert. I have signed up to take riding lessons and will be going to Georgia soon to hike with my son. A week away will hopefully refresh me mentally, emotionally and physically."

Barbara Link – New River Valley Pet Sitting & Farm Services, LLC Christiansburg, Virginia

Action Steps – Exercise More Effectively

Action Step

Choose a regular movement exercise you can do for at least 30 minutes each day by yourself. This is a time for reflection and creativity, so choose a repetitive action that does not require too much mental focus. Commit to doing this exercise every day for two weeks. During your exercise, let your mind wander. Some days you may think of something specific, others you may think about nothing at all. As ideas come to you, write them down on your phone or in a small journal. For an even more powerful experience, combine this activity with writing Morning Pages. At the end of the two weeks, record how you feel about this special brainstorming time and what ideas have come to you during the exercise.

Action Step

Go back and read through the "Tips for Fitting Exercise into a Busy Schedule" section again and select at least two tips to try this week. In your burnout recovery journal, write down which tips you plan to follow and how you plan to do so.

For example, if you choose the first tip, you might write something like this in your journal:

Figure out what works best for you: I will try exercising in the morning, afternoon and at night for two days each and see which works better for my day. I will find at least two workout videos or routines to follow as well as a place near home I can hike or walk. At the end of the week, I will decide which exercises I enjoyed and which I did not.

Action Step

Set a movement goal for yourself. This may be a fitness or strength goal, but it does not need to be. It may also be as simple as a daily step count or taking a walk after dinner each evening. Whatever your goal is, write it down and post it in a place where you will see it often.

Part Five

Moving Forward in Your Burnout Recovery

"If your compassion does not include yourself, it is incomplete."

–Jack Kornfield

SEVENTEEN

Going the Speed of Your Soul

Find, and Follow, Your Own Ideal Pace

"In an age of acceleration, nothing can be more exhilarating than going slow."

–Pico Iyer

One of my favorite authors is Parker Palmer, a Quaker, educator and activist. He has written and spoken extensively about the importance of going at the pace, or speed, of our souls. This idea is especially important for pet professionals recovering from, and trying to avoid, burnout.

If you're on social media, you've probably seen the terms "word porn" or "food porn," but a term that gained massive popularity during the pandemic was this: "productivity porn."

During the pandemic, it seemed everyone was baking bread, knitting sweaters and growing veggies from the tops of their recently eaten veggies — plus so much more!

Whew. I felt exhausted just seeing all those creations popping up all over social media.

Don't get me wrong, I love being productive. I am an ambitious person by nature and I definitely like getting stuff done, checking items off my to-do list and accomplishing tasks. It's a fantastic feeling. Going from a fast-paced life to a slower one is not always an easy thing, which is probably why there was so much "productivity porn" during the shelter-in-place time.

But slowing down is often required when it comes to the speed of soul. As much as I enjoy taking action, my soul requires that I balance all that productivity with a slower, easier pace as well.

It's Okay to Just Be

Most of us have become people who are busy doing but aren't comfortable *just being*. If we weren't this way before starting a business, many become that way after starting a business. Running a business often requires having attention on many different aspects of the business. This can lead to a sense of feeling like we must always be doing something. For some of us, this busyness is tied to our very sense of self-worth and often it indicates an unconscious belief of "If I'm not productive, I'm not valuable, worthy or perhaps even lovable."

> AS MUCH AS I ENJOY TAKING ACTION, MY SOUL REQUIRES THAT I BALANCE ALL THAT PRODUCTIVITY WITH A SLOWER PACE AS WELL.

For others, being busy can become an addiction—a way to not feel painful feelings and to numb the parts of being human that hurt when we feel emotions like disappointment, fear, anger, etc.

For me, the speed of my soul is nearly always much slower than the pace of my regular daily life. I get energized and even amped up when I'm working on a few projects at a time. When I am working quickly between them all, I'm like a bee flitting from flower to flower and that's often a happy experience for me.

However, when I'm done with work on those projects for the day or week, it can then be challenging to slow (the heck) down and get into the rhythm of my soul when I've been revving full speed ahead to complete or tie up loose ends on my passion projects or business tasks.

And yet, going the speed of my soul—even for an hour or two—is often exactly what I need in order to recharge, revamp and revitalize. When I fail to do so, I find myself running on fumes, which results in me being much less effective in my work. I also find I am much less of a human being and instead am a "human doing" with those I interact with throughout the day. I've learned that creating space and time to go the speed of my soul is crucial for me to fill my well and to be able to burn on all eight internal and external cylinders when it's time to dive into my projects again.

How I Go the Speed of My Soul

Each person's soul pace is different, but as a business coach I've talked to many entrepreneurs and pet professionals and I have noticed a few common trends. In this chapter, I've included what I've found to work for me, and at the end of this chapter, you'll read stories of other pet business owners for you to use as inspiration while you find your own soul speed and rhythm.

Here are some ways I bring the speed of soul into my personal life and my business and how you can do the same:

Nearly every month I go on a solo work retreat for three to four days to a remote house in the woods in California.

Before I leave on each monthly work trip, I create a short list of important work tasks I want to complete while on my work retreat. I often get all of them done, and sometimes even many more tasks done, in an easy and relaxed way because this large amount of undisturbed time to focus my attention and energy gives me the space to do just that.

Because the house is so remote, bringing all the food I will need while I'm there is crucial unless I want to drive 45 minutes to a grocery store (which I never want to do). So, on the way to my work retreat, I stop at my favorite grocery store and get pre-packaged healthy salads and soups to last me the entire time. Not having to cook meals gives me even more time and space to focus on work while also eating very healthy while I'm away.

I often "go feral" while there — I usually work from bed and in my pajamas and only get up for bio breaks and to eat my pre-made food! It's a blissful experience, and the work I accomplish during those few days' time is often the best work of my entire month.

Even though I'm working, I'm absolutely going the speed of my soul. My soul doesn't want to get dressed (my soul loves being feral). My soul doesn't want to prepare meals (at least not while on my work retreat). It wants to be a bit wild and perhaps not take a shower for a day or two and instead focus single-handedly on the task that's right in front of me in that particular moment in time (which, by the way, is also what I'm doing now — writing this chapter from my bed while on my work retreat).

Do I take a shower after a day or two? Absolutely. In fact, I often do bathe daily but usually in the form of a long, leisurely relaxing bath (which is what my soul really wants... my soul loves baths, especially baths in the work retreat house big bathtub).

My suggestion for you: If you're finding yourself yearning to go the speed of your soul and you want to figure out what and how that might look for you, I encourage you to schedule your own work retreat.

Maybe your work retreat is only spending 24 hours away because of your personal or business obligations. Perhaps if 24 hours goes well, then you extend your retreat the following month to 48 hours. Or perhaps you schedule a three-day work retreat once every quarter. My version of what works for me may be very different from what yours looks like for you, and that's okay!

Even if scheduling a work retreat feels impossible due to time or money (or both), I encourage you to begin exploring short-term rental spots now that could perhaps be ideal work retreat spots in the future. Then, when you're ready to schedule your retreat, you've got a ready-made list of possibilities to choose from.

If a quiet environment or a bathtub are very important to you (they both are for me), then messaging the short-term rental host now to inquire about the noise factor or bathroom facilities might help you either eliminate a particular choice now, or if it seems ideal, you can bookmark it as a possible spot to schedule your future work retreat.

> **Burnout Recovery Tip**
> If your work or personal schedule require a work retreat that is more of a spontaneous experience, then having a "go bag" pre-packed and ready to go and downloading apps that have last-minute hotel or resort deals could be a good fit for you.

Another way I go the speed of my soul is by making my morning routine a sacred and non-negotiable practice—no matter what is going on in my life or where I am in the world. Even if I have to shorten my morning routine from the usual 45 minutes, having that quiet time with myself, my journal, and my soul in the morning, before my work-day begins, is crucial for my well-being and often positively impacts the entire day.

My suggestion for you: Decide now that your morning routine is sacred and necessary. All of the suggestions in Chapter Eleven can help you design a truly rejuvenating morning, but only if you carve out the time for it every (or almost every) day.

Another way to quickly bring myself to the speed of my soul is remembering that the people in my life are *the most important* facet of my life and taking action to show them that they are important is crucial for my well-being. That's not to say that switching gears from work to engaging with my friends and family is always easy. I love my work and can get consumed by it—but when my loved ones, including my husband, feel like I'm neglecting them, I know it's time to pick my head up from my computer and truly connect with the humans who matter most to me. Sometimes physically putting my computer away in a closet or a drawer helps me disengage from my work and creates the transition to connection with loved ones.

My suggestion for you: Let your loved ones be a barometer for how well you are balancing work with your personal life. This might mean having a conversation about what they need from you, or maybe you simply need to be more aware of times you need to put away your work and truly focus on those you love.

Going on walks without my phone is a sure-fire way to get me to slow down internally, but it doesn't often happen without internal reservations. (What if I see something I want to take a picture of? What if the friend or family member I've been wanting to talk to calls me, etc.?) But when I do leave my phone at home and foot it without, I feel better. I can feel my nervous system begin to regulate and go from speedy and anxious to slow and peaceful.

My suggestion for you: Disconnect regularly, even if only for short periods of time. Learn to untether yourself from your phone and let your soul set the pace of a walk, a nap, a conversation or whatever activity you're completing phone-free.

Burnout Recovery Success Stories

"Going the speed of my soul means I acknowledge where I am mentally, emotionally and spiritually. When I reach burnout, it means I haven't been taking care of myself. I need to evaluate what has caused me to get off track, so I do a self-inventory of my mind, emotions and spirit.

I ask myself these questions when I feel myself going faster than the speed of my soul:

Mental:

When did I stop learning new things?

When did I stop reading and researching?

When did I stop challenging myself to learn more technology?

Emotional:

HALT: Am I hungry, angry, lonely or tired? My body chemistry changes when I am in HALT.

Am I keeping up with my physical activity?

Am I setting up emotional boundaries? Remember, NO is a complete sentence.

Spiritual:

How much time do I invest with daily prayer and meditation? Am I keeping up with my yoga practice?

Have I been attending church and my Bible study regularly?

Am I selfless and doing random acts of kindness? Do I practice kindness with my family and friends?

In addition to these self-reflections, I have learned to use throughout the years, my husband and I started a new tradition recently: coffee and crosswords. We make a date to go to a local coffee shop and while at the coffee shop, we do a crossword puzzle. We have found that crosswords get our brain juices moving. It's very stimulating and connecting!"
Julie André - The DIVAS Pet Sitters, LLC
Mandeville, Louisiana

"The topic of 'going the speed of soul' brings up many things for me that I'm so passionate about! One thing in particular: I recently read a quote by Kate Northrup that says, 'Your worth is not determined by how much you get done.' I think for so many years (decades even), I have become accustomed to basing my worth on how much work I get done or how busy I am. I can so easily get wrapped up in that way of thinking. Head down and plow through! Don't get me wrong, hard work is an important part of life, but measuring my self-worth based on the amount of work I get done or how busy I am is just setting myself up for disappointment. For me, it sets me

up for feeling restless, irritable and discontent. It puts me in a fight or flight mode. I want off that train! It does not serve me. And it doesn't allow me to be of service to others.

As an entrepreneur, it is easy to become obsessed with work, leaving little to no time for self-care. When I put self-care first, I am able to show up in my business refreshed, focused, energized, creative, driven, encouraging... all the things I want to be! And the business succeeds because of it!

Going the speed of soul means aligning my will with my higher power. A higher power is whatever you define it to be. For me, my higher power changes over time. When I'm not going the speed of soul and not aligning my will with my higher power, I'm burned out, tired, depressed, sad, in self-pity, comparing myself and my company to others. I isolate myself and my business suffers because I have nothing left to give. I'm ready to give up, put in the towel and just run away forever!

I'm very lucky to have a big support system in my life. I heard a friend share about her support system — she called them her 'mattresses.' Now, I visualize myself falling onto these comfy, cozy mattresses when I need support. I have them in my personal and professional life. Sometimes it's really easy to ask for help and lean on my mattresses. Sometimes it's really hard, especially if I am in the thick of it and it doesn't feel like things will ever change. But it's in those times where picking up the phone is the most important! That phone may feel like it's a thousand pounds, but if I want to get back on track, I have to pick it up and call the person and talk to them. If that person doesn't answer, I move on to the next. I feel a hundred times better when I do. Then, I get into action! I write a list of things I am grateful for, take a walk, take a bath, meditate... Notice none of these are business related! The bottom line is, in these moments where I am just really bummed out, I'm often only thinking about how I am being affected. It can help to get out of myself, get out of my head and do something for someone else. Even just calling a friend to ask how they are doing helps me slow down and go the speed of my soul.

I'll leave you with this: don't be driven by fear! Fear is just when we are 'Forgetting Everything's All Right!'"

Michelle Sabia - Paws & Claws Pet Sitting Services
Cave Creek, Arizona & Litchfield, Connecticut

Action Steps – Going the Speed of Your Soul

Action Step

What is the speed of *your* soul? Discover the answer through journal writing. Free write for three pages about this topic and/or use the following questions designed to help you begin to customize a "speed of soul tool kit" you can fall back on when you're going too fast and doing too much:

What does "going the speed of soul" look like and mean for me?

What helps me get back into balance in order to be a human being instead of a "human doing"?

Does a work retreat sound like something that would be beneficial for me and if so, when and where would I like to go?

What is something simple I can do today to begin to get back into work/life balance?

Are there particular things I've noticed get me off balance (for example: lack of sleep, excessive alcohol or sugar intake, not having enough alone time if I'm an introvert, not having enough social time if I'm an extrovert, etc.)?

What are some actions I can take starting today to help me get back on track to go the speed of my soul?

Action Step

In the "How I Go the Speed of My Soul" section, I outlined four specific ways I go the speed of my soul and suggestions for how you can do the same in your life.

Read through that section and the *Burnout Recovery Success Stories* again, this time with your burnout recovery journal open and ready. As you read what works for me and other pet professionals, write down any ideas you think might be a good fit for you. These ideas will act as a resource for you as you find your own speed of soul.

EIGHTEEN

The End (for Now)

Enjoy the Benefits of Burnout Recovery and Prevent Future Burnout

"Burnout, compassion fatigue and moral distress have differing causes but similar symptoms and effective ways to prevent and treat them all. Caregivers deserve nothing less."

–Carla Cheatham

As you read the final pages of this book, I hope you already feel a lightening of your load and a decrease in burnout and stress. However, if you still feel overwhelmed and exhausted, don't get discouraged—burnout recovery can take time and some deep, intentional work. Just keep at it! Soon enough, the habits of self-care, partnering with your body and setting boundaries with your business and clients will become easier and more natural. Perhaps, like me, you will soon experience your own Year of Radical Change.

Whether you've completely revolutionized your relationship with your business or are just tentatively starting to make changes, take a moment now, at the end of this book, to think about what you've learned about yourself and about the process of healing from burnout. Chances are good you are starting to experience the benefits of burnout recovery already.

Looking Ahead to the Benefits of Burnout Recovery

Now that you have recovered from your burnout—or are on the path to recovery—there are many benefits you will probably start to notice in your life.

Here are just some of the benefits of burnout recovery experienced by other pet professionals who have gone through the steps in this book:

- Creating a schedule that includes a rich personal life
- The ability to "turn off your business" and just be you
- Better physical and emotional health
- Enthusiasm and time for hobbies and projects
- Opportunities and time to travel
- Closer and more meaningful personal relationships

How many of those benefits have you already experienced in your burnout recovery since starting this book? Recognizing these benefits will help you continue your efforts to heal from burnout—and to prevent burnout in the future.

Preventing Burnout in the Future

Burnout can have many causes, including stress from a lot of success. At the beginning of the book, I told you about a time I experienced a second round of burnout, even after I'd recovered from burnout years before and thought I'd tamed that monster and it would never return. Even when you reach a point of peace and balance and feel ready to move on from burnout recovery, there may be a time in the future when you need the resources in this book again.

This is the end of the book, but not the end of your personal and business burnout recovery. Many times throughout these chapters, I've encouraged you to really dig deep and honestly evaluate yourself and your business, in order to create change. If you've taken me up on that challenge, your burnout recovery journal will be a resource to you moving forward. It is likely full of ideas, goals and thoughts you've had throughout the reading of this book. Use the journal entries as guideposts along your own personal burnout recovery roadmap.

Following this chapter, you will find a *Reading List* and *Recommended Resources*. Both sections are designed to give you additional guidance and support as you continue through your burnout recovery and in the future, if you feel the need to come back to these pages and discover again how to step back from overwhelm and into peace.

And finally, when you are feeling burned out, I encourage you to remember:

You have enough.

You do enough.

You are enough.

Reading List

Reading the perspectives of others has been essential in my own burnout recovery and prevention, as well as in my own personal growth journey. I encourage you to start your own essential reading list with the books you find most helpful.

If you need a place to start, I heartily recommend these books:

Addiction to Perfection by Marion Woodman

Balancing Heaven and Earth: A Memoir of Visions, Dreams and Realizations by Robert A. Johnson and Jerry M. Ruhl

The Artist's Way: A Spiritual Path to Higher Creativity by Julia Cameron

Digital Minimalism: Choosing a Focused Life in a Noisy World by Cal Newport

Essentialism: The Disciplined Pursuit of Less by Greg McKeown

First, We Make the Beast Beautiful: A New Story About Anxiety by Sarah Wilson

The Four Tendencies: The Indispensable Personality Profiles That Reveal How to Make Your Life Better (and Other People's Lives Better, Too) by Gretchen Rubin

The Fringe Hours: Making Time for You by Jessica N. Turner

The Gifts of Imperfection: Let Go of Who You Think You're Supposed to Be and Embrace Who You Are by Brené Brown

How to Do Nothing: Resisting the Attention Economy by Jenny Odell

Inner Work: Using Dreams and Active Imagination for Personal Growth by Robert A. Johnson

Let Your Life Speak: Listening for the Voice of Vocation by Parker Palmer

A Hidden Wholeness: The Journey Toward an Undivided Life by Parker Palmer

Meditation for Fidgety Skeptics by Dan Harris

Memories, Dreams, Reflections by C.G. Jung

Modern Man in Search of a Soul by C.G. Jung

Present Over Perfect: Leaving Behind Frantic for a Simpler, More Soulful Way of Living by Shauna Niequist

Quiet: The Power of Introverts in a World That Can't Stop Talking by Susan Cain

The Red Book: Liber Novus by C.G. Jung

Sabbath: Finding Rest, Renewal, and Delight in Our Busy Lives by Wayne Muller

Tired But Wired: How to Overcome Sleep Problems: The Essential Sleep Toolkit by Nerina Ramlakhan

Recommended Resources

Please note: these resources are listed by chapter. Not every chapter in the book needed external resources, so you may notice some "missing" chapters below. You may also find resources recommended for one topic that are helpful for your burnout recovery in another way. As with every part of your burnout recovery and prevention, finding what works for you is more important than following all of these recommendations.

Chapter Four: Take the "Busy" Out of Your Business

Administration Software: Administration software programs specific to pet care can help you automate much of the behind-the-scenes work of running a pet business. Email me at **thrive@SFPBacademy.com** if you want my software recommendation.

Google Voice: Google Voice is a popular VoIP (Voice over Internet Protocol) option among business owners for good reason. You can choose a phone number with almost any area code and port calls and texts to your computer or personal phone. **voice.google.com**

Ooma: Another VoIP I highly recommend (and have used personally) is Ooma. When I make calls with the Ooma app, my business number will show up on people's caller ID, allowing me to keep my personal number private. **ooma.com**

SimplyBook: This online booking system, designed specifically for service-based businesses, can be used alone or incorporated with your business website and social media platforms. **simplybook.me**

Square Appointments: Square Appointments combines booking and payments into one service. You can even use it to charge cancellation fees automatically. **squareup.com/appointments**

The Association for Pet Loss and Bereavement: This nonprofit organization specializes in helping people through the grief of losing a pet through a chat room, memorials and other resources. **aplb.org**

Goodbye, Friend: Healing Wisdom for Anyone Who Has Ever Lost a Pet: This book by Gary Kowalski can be a comfort to you or your clients when dealing with the loss of a beloved pet. **kowalskibooks.com**

Pet Loss Support: The University of Florida College of Veterinary Medicine maintains a website all about pet loss support that includes links to online resources for grieving pet owners, pet loss hotlines and articles about specific topics such as how to help other pets adjust and self-care during the grieving process. **smallanimal.vethospital.ufl.edu/resources/pet-loss-support**

DocuSign: An all-electronic signature and contract service, DocuSign helps keep your contracts and agreements organized and available remotely on the cloud. **docusign.com**

Freedom: Freedom is an app that allows you to block the internet or certain websites and apps on your phone and computer during specific times of day or days of the week. **freedom.to**

HelloSign: HelloSign offers a full line of electronic contracts, e-signature options and mobile forms you can customize for your business. **hellosign.com**

Chapter Six: Be a Conscientious Steward of Your Money

FreshBooks: If your accounting or point-of-sale app does not have an invoicing option, FreshBooks will let you create and send professional invoices from your phone. **freshbooks.com**

Hootsuite: As you organize your content calendar, Hootsuite enables you to schedule your posts in advance so you can have your updates, articles and links all lined up ahead of time. **hootsuite.com**

Post Planner: This one is super easy to use for your Facebook and Twitter accounts. It also has some suggested content and you'll find inspirational memes you can use on your own social media accounts. **postplanner.com**

Rate Increase Letter: If you haven't increased your prices in a while, or if you need suggestions on the best ways to notify your clients of the price increase, you will find a sample rate increase email template at the bottom of the "Free Stuff" page of my website: **SFPBacademy.com/free**

Sendible: Sendible is a social media software program with a search feature, trending keywords, content curation, social media scheduling and a rotating list for your content. **sendible.com**

Chapter Seven: Master Your Time

Focusmate: Focusmate pairs you with an accountability co-working partner online for 50-minute sessions which allows you to enjoy the benefits of personal accountability remotely. It's perfect for maintaining accountability for personal and self-care activities (cooking, exercise, meditation, etc.) as well as countless business tasks. There's also a Focusmate group especially for pet business owners! **focusmate.com/signup/ProsperousPetBusiness**

Forest: If you need extra incentive to stay focused, the Forest app breaks your work into manageable chunks and provides a visual representation of your efforts with achievements and rewards. **forestapp.cc**

Moment: The Moment app tracks and limits daily phone usage to help you avoid the "rabbit hole" of social media when you need to be working. **inthemoment.io**

Productive: This goal-setting app lets you input specific deadlines and milestones for each goal. **productiveapp.io**

Productivity Challenge Timer: The Productivity Challenge Timer works on the Pomodoro method, encouraging 20-minute periods of focus followed by short breaks in between work sessions. The app is designed specifically to make maintaining your productivity feel like a game, tapping into the fun and reward of achieving smaller goals and ranks. **productivitychallengetimer.com**

Roam Research: Keep track of your schedule, ideas and notes in one virtual place. **roamresearch.com**

Smart Home: A smart home system lets you connect your thermostat and appliances virtually, allowing you to control everything from a single app or device. As mentioned in the book, this kind of streamlining and automation can free up your time and energy for more important tasks. Many smart home systems also incorporate a router, giving you total control of your internet and home in one place. Google Home, Samsung Hub and Eufy Smart Home are three popular options for setting up a smart home.

Strides Habit Tracker: This is another popular goal-setting app for setting and tracking effective goals. **stridesapp.com**

Trello: Trello is a productivity app, designed entirely around the idea of making organizing ideas fun, flexible and easy for all. You can work together with a team or individually and have access to your lists and idea boards on the go. **trello.com**

Toggl: Track how you spend your time quickly and easily with Toggl, which has plenty of functionality in the free version and browser extensions for Chrome and Firefox so you can seamlessly track your time spent online as well. **toggl.com**

Chapter Eight: Hire and Manage Staff

Application Packet: My fully customizable Application Packet for Hiring Pet Sitters and Dog Walkers is available on my website. **SFPBacademy.com/packet**

Hours: This time-tracking app makes it easy for you to keep track of what you do (and how long it takes) on any given workday. This is especially helpful for figuring out what to ask your office managers to do for you... and about how long it will take once they learn how to do it. You can even add notes to specific activities, making it even simpler to train your staff on a particular job. **hourstimetracking.com**

Nextdoor: Finding local help for everyday tasks such as landscaping, housework and laundry services is made simple with Nextdoor or another neighborhood social media group. You will get some of the best recommendations from neighbors who are already using these services or may offer the service themselves. **nextdoor.com**

Office Manager Hiring Kit: A comprehensive hiring kit for office managers and administrative assistants that includes a customizable job posting, application packet and manager manual that you can customize for your business needs. **SFPSA.com/manager**

TaskRabbit: TaskRabbit specializes in connecting you with same-day services, such as a local handyman, cleaning companies and help running errands. **taskrabbit.com**

Chapter Nine: Personalize Your Rest

16 Personalities: This is a particularly easy-to-use resource for finding and understanding your Meyers-Briggs personality type, which can be a key part of figuring out your own specific needs as you personalize your rest. You can find in-depth analysis and suggestions for each personality type and how to better handle the personal and professional challenges associated with each. **16personalities.com**

Jung Society of Washington: The Jung Society of Washington offers online programs and a list of resources for anyone looking to learn more about the work of Carl Jung. **jung.org**

Quiet: The Power of Introverts in a World That Can't Stop Talking: This book by Susan Cain is a great resource for introverts and anyone who wants to understand them better. The author also hosts a podcast about navigating specific aspects of life as (or with) an introvert. **quietrev.com**

Chapter Ten: Calm Your Mind and the Rest Will Follow

Calm: With meditations as short as three minutes, Calm is designed to make meditation accessible in any schedule. The app also includes tools for better sleep, like stories, sounds and music to help you sleep. **calm.com**

Freedom: Freedom is an app that allows you to block the internet or certain websites and apps on your phone and computer during specific times of day or days of the week. **freedom.to**

Headspace: Headspace offers helpful how-tos and information about sleep, stress, meditation and mindfulness on the website. The app features guided meditations, SOS meditations for emergency situations, sleep sounds and more. **headspace.com**

Hootsuite: Schedule your posts in advance using Hootsuite so you can completely disconnect from social media except for when you are actively preparing business posts and updates. **hootsuite.com**

Insight Timer: Insight Timer is an app that walks you through guided meditation as you meditate and improve your mindfulness. **insighttimer.com**

RescueTime: You can load RescueTime on your computer and phone and view a daily report of how much time you spend on each site online. You also have the option to restrict access to specific sites if you need help cutting a time-wasting habit. **rescuetime.com**

Ten Percent Happier: The Ten Percent Happier app and podcast both focus on meditation and practical advice for a happier, healthier you. **tenpercent.com**

TRE: TRE is an innovative series of exercises that assist the body in releasing deep muscular patterns of stress, tension and trauma. The exercises safely activate a natural reflex mechanism of shaking or vibrating that releases muscular tension, calming down the nervous system. When this muscular shaking/vibrating mechanism is activated in a safe and controlled environment, the body is encouraged to return back to a state of balance. **traumaprevention.com**

Chapter Eleven: Reclaim Your Morning

Insight Timer: Many morning routines include meditation and mindfulness. Insight Timer is an app that walks you through guided meditation as you meditate and improve your mindfulness. **insighttimer.com**

My Morning Routine: Developed from the book, *My Morning Routine: How Successful People Start Every Day Inspired* by Benjamin Spall and Michael Xander, the My Morning Routine website is full of over 300 morning routines from successful professionals all over the world, categorized by job type, early bird or night owl, morning routines for parents and more. **mymorningroutine.com**

Chapter Fourteen: Food as Fuel

Ate: This mindful eating app is not focused on tracking calories, but rather on helping you reach your goals by focusing on what you ate and how it made you feel. **youate.com**

MyFitnessPal: MyFitnessPal is a free online and mobile calorie counter and diet plan you can use to track what you eat using your own information or searching the worldwide database of foods and recipes submitted by other users. **myfitnesspal.com**

Noom: The Noom app takes a behavioral approach to lifestyle changes and weight loss and can help you build healthier habits. **noom.com**

Productive: This goal-setting app lets you input specific deadlines and milestones for each goal and can be helpful as you make changes to your dietary habits. **productiveapp.io**

WaterMinder: Use this app to quickly log your water intake and stay hydrated during your busy day. WaterMinder syncs with other iOS health apps and is also available for Android phones. **waterminder.com**

Strides Habit Tracker: This is another popular goal-setting app for setting and tracking effective goals. **stridesapp.com**

Chapter Fifteen: Savor Sleep

Calm: With meditations as short as three minutes, Calm is designed to make meditation accessible in any schedule. The app also includes tools for better sleep, like stories, sounds and music to help you sleep. **calm.com**

F.lux: F.lux automatically adjusts the light on your computer and phone throughout the day to be warmer as it gets closer to evening to help you avoid blue light at night so you can sleep better. **justgetflux.com**

Headspace: Headspace offers helpful how-tos and information about sleep, stress, meditation and mindfulness on the website. The app features guided meditations, SOS meditations for emergency situations, sleep sounds and more. **headspace.com**

Sleep Cycle: Sleep Cycle tracks and analyzes your sleep and wakes you up at the ideal point of your sleep cycle within the desired window you set before you go to bed. **sleepcycle.com**

Chapter Sixteen: Exercise More Effectively

GoogleFit: GoogleFit, which is available for both iOS and Android devices, was developed with the help of the American Heart Association and focuses on encouraging you to set (and work toward) fitness goals. **google.com/fit**

MyFitnessPal: MyFitnessPal is not just for tracking what you eat; it has a step-tracking feature as well. You can use the app to track your movement by itself or sync it with a smart watch, if you have one. **myfitnesspal.com**

PEAR: The PEAR app is a health and fitness platform designed to function like a trainer in your pocket, letting you get a high-quality workout from home or on the road. **pearsports.com**

Productive: This goal-setting app lets you input specific deadlines and milestones for each goal, which can be a big motivator when starting a new exercise routine. **productiveapp.io**

7 Minute Workout: The 7 Minute Workout Challenge App contains a collection of high intensity workouts that take just seven minutes a day. **7minworkoutapp.net**

SIX-FIGURE
PET BUSINESS ACADEMY™
launch. expand. thrive.

Tools and Programs to Help You Achieve Pet Business Success... NOW!

Throughout your burnout recovery and moving forward, here are some tools and programs that provide additional support to you, the business owner, as you nurture your pet business.

Pet Business Coaching with Kristin Morrison

Are you ready to take your business to the next level but need support to help you do that? I can help you take your business where you want it to go, quickly and easily. I've helped thousands of pet business owners from around the world, and I can definitely help you with whatever challenges you face with your pet business.

Visit my business coaching page for testimonials and to sign up for business coaching with me: **www.SFPBacademy.com/coach**

Search Engine Optimization (SEO) Coaching

In just one complete session, I can take most pet business websites from low (or non-existent) on search engine results to much higher — often to page one.

Visit the SEO coaching page to find out more: **www.SFPSA.com/seo**

Tools for Start-Up, Growth, Acceleration and Hiring

Thousands of pet professionals from all over the world have used the Six-Figure Pet Sitting Academy™ Pet Sitting and Dog Walking Start-Up Kit, client contracts, hiring tools and success recordings to start and grow their pet businesses. And you can too!

The page listed below contains over 50 pet business forms and tools that can help you get started or expand your business — right now!

All products are available for instant download, so you'll receive the items you order in less than 60 seconds. Also, all start-up and hiring kits, client contracts and forms are fully editable so you can customize as needed for your business.

Find out more about the products that can take your pet business to the next level:

www.SFPSA.com/petsit

4-Week Pet Business Online Group Programs

Do you need support to create a profitable and easy-to-run business *and* a great life?

I offer online pet business programs, and you are welcome to join me and other pet professionals from around the world who are excited to create a successful business and fulfilling life. Each program has a private Facebook group to keep you connected and feeling supported long after the programs are over.

These are virtual programs, and they are designed so you can participate from anywhere in the world. You can even attend from your office or from your car! And if you miss a class, no problem—the recording will be available for you to watch, listen and learn from whenever you like.

The **Catapult 4-Week Pet Business Bootcamp** is for professionals who want to launch their business into greater success with ease.

The **Jumpstart 4-Week Pet Business Burnout Recovery Program** is a recovery course for pet business owners suffering from pet business burnout (you know who you are).

The **30 Days to Start and Grow Your Pet Sitting and Dog Walking Business Program** is designed for anyone who wants to take the dream of owning a pet business from idea to reality in 30 days, within the supportive and accountable framework of a weekly course, surrounded by like-minded pet business entrepreneurs who really "get it."

You can learn more about the online programs, read testimonials from past graduates and sign up now by visiting the pages below:

Six-Figure Pet Business Academy Online Course Learning Platform:

Explore the "anytime 24/7 access" online courses for pet business owners:

www.learn.SFPBacademy.com

Catapult 4-Week Pet Business Bootcamp:

www.SFPSA.com/catapult

Jumpstart 4-Week Pet Business Burnout Recovery Program:

www.SFPSA.com/jump

30 Days to Start and Grow Your Pet Business Online Program:

www.SFPSA.com/30

More Money. More Ease. More Freedom!

Prosperous Pet Business Podcast

Each month, I release podcast episodes to help you in your pet business journey (and in your personal life). There are a lot of podcast episodes already available and waiting for you, and they are all free. Check them out!

You can listen by subscribing on your favorite podcast service or by visiting the Prosperous Pet Business podcast page:

www.prosperouspetbusiness.com/pet-business-podcast

Prosperous Pet Business Online Conference

Every year, I interview pet business experts and offer those valuable interviews for FREE at an annual online conference that is just for pet business owners. Find out more and sign up here:

www.prosperouspetbusiness.com

FREE Six-Figure Pet Sitting Academy™ Resources

Find a free sample rate increase letter plus many other no-cost items to help you on the Six-Figure Pet Business Academy "Free Stuff" page:

www.SFPBacademy.com/free

Visit the Six-Figure Pet Business Academy™ blog for business tips, tools and articles on how to create a pet business beyond your wildest dreams!

www.sixfigurepetbusinessacademy.com/blog

Sign up for the FREE Six-Figure Business Tips and Tools Newsletter:

www.SFPBacademy.com

I would love to hear how this book has helped you find more balance and peace as you recover from pet business burnout.

Email me your burnout recovery success story:
thrive@SFPBacademy.com

Connect with me and Six-Figure Pet Business Academy on these social media sites:

Follow me on Facebook:
Facebook.com/SixFigurePetSittingAcademy

Join the Facebook group for readers of this book:
Facebook.com/groups/RecoverFromPetBusinessBurnout

Join my private Facebook group with pet business owners from all over the world: Facebook.com/groups/ProsperousPetBusiness

Instagram: Instagram.com/PetBizCoach

LinkedIn: LinkedIn.com/in/SixFigurePetSitting

Pinterest: Pinterest.com/SixFigurePetBiz

Twitter: Twitter.com/PetBizCoach

Appreciation

This book is a result of so many who helped birth it into being. I'm grateful for each and every one of you.

First, though it is not often done, I want to thank the three places this book was written. I believe the location(s) in which a book is written impact a book's "soul." I wrote this book in Marin County, Big Sur and Hawaii. Like many writers, I require large periods of solitude in order to write. Writing a book can be challenging, but having these three beautiful, peaceful and quiet spots to write this book made the job of writing it easier and pleasurable.

Thank you so much to this book's early readers. I received valuable feedback from each of you on what needed to be added, changed and adjusted before this book could be released. Your suggestions were invaluable.

Huge gratitude to the many pet business owners from around the world who contributed to the "burnout recovery success stories" in this book. Your many important and relevant real-life stories bring this book to life in a powerful, potent way.

Those of you who are my past or present coaching clients are a big part of why I wrote this book. Many of you have struggled with burnout and have brought that struggle to your coaching sessions. It's been an honor and a pleasure to work with you using the processes contained within this book and, as a result of your willingness to "work it," to then see you go on to create rich personal lives and fall in love with your businesses. The most heartwarming part for me has been witnessing you make time for, and deepen relationships with, your family and friends, as well as rekindle a loving relationship with yourself.

As always, thank you to my Thursday Afternoon Business Group. You've been a constant, solid support that has held me steady, especially in the midst of this swirling year of change. From the bottom of my heart: thank you.

Thank you to my wonderful editor and wordsmith extraordinaire, Kimberly M. Your tireless work is absolutely why this book is here today! I appreciate so much about your contribution but especially how you consistently manage to keep my voice in the midst of the editing process.

And finally, deep appreciation to my husband, Spencer. You are the love of my life and my greatest support. I am certain I wouldn't have met you had I not gotten off the "overworking train." The possibility of meeting you was my greatest motivator to stop overworking. I'm so glad I listened to the wise part of me that knew I'd have to stop investing so much energy and time into work and instead create some blank space in order for you to arrive. Thank you for your unwavering support and love. You mean the world to me.

About the Author

Kristin Morrison started her pet sitting and dog walking company in 1995 and it grew to be one of the largest pet care companies in California. She hired over 250 pet sitters and dog walkers during the course of running her business. When she sold her business in 2013, it had grown to include 35 staff members and 4 managers.

Since 2000, Kristin has provided pet business coaching for thousands of pet sitters, dog walkers and other service-based pet business owners across the United States, Canada, the UK and Australia. In 2008, she founded Six-Figure Pet Sitting Academy™, which provides coaching, webinars and business products for pet sitters and dog walkers. She also created Six-Figure Pet Business Academy™ for all service-based pet business owners, including dog trainers, pet groomers and dog daycare owners.

Kristin is a nationally recognized speaker at pet business conferences and for pet business networking groups. She also hosts the annual Prosperous Pet Business Online Conference and the Prosperous Pet Business podcast. Kristin has written five additional books for pet business owners: *The Hiring Handbook for Pet Sitters and Dog Walkers, 30 Days to Start and Grow Your Pet Sitting and Dog Walking Business, Six-Figure Pet Sitting, Prosperous Pet Business* and *Six-Figure Pet Business*. Kristin lives in Northern California and Hawaii with her husband, Spencer.

CPSIA information can be obtained
at www.ICGtesting.com
Printed in the USA
BVHW081728060421
604327BV00014B/891

9 780997 872866